T0167161

A Delicate Task

Teaching and Learning
on a Montessori Path

Catherine McTamaney, Ed.D.

A Delicate Task
Teaching and Learning on a Montessori Path

iUniverse books may be ordered through booksellers or by contacting:

iUniverse
1663 Liberty Drive
Bloomington, IN 47403
www.iuniverse.com
844-349-9409

Cover design by Robert Grossman, 2012

ISBN: 978-1-4759-3142-6 (sc)
ISBN: 978-1-4759-3144-0 (hc)
ISBN: 978-1-4759-3143-3 (e)

Library of Congress Control Number: 2012910100

Print information available on the last page.

iUniverse rev. date: 06/18/2024

For Sister Leonor J. Esnard, OP, PhD

Scientist and Artist

FOREWORD
Marie M. Dugan

Based on the lifetime work of Maria Montessori, "A Delicate Task," tackles Montessori's series of eleven qualities unique to human existence. Dr. Montessori named them Orientation, Order, Exploration, Communication, Activity, Manipulation, Work, Repetition, Precision, Abstraction, and Perfection: those qualities that defined and distinguished our development across lifetimes, cultures and generations. In "A Delicate Task," Catherine matches the Montessori Prepared Environment to each tendency, and the needs of the child. Each tendency is addressed in its own chapter, and each chapter is organized into four parts.

Here is where the magic happens. One by one, page by page, the Montessori Method enfolds. By understanding the Tendencies, a new understanding of the Montessori Method emerges. I found myself in meditation at the end of each chapter. The focus throughout is the child. No distractions, no conclusions, just a beautiful journey into the happenings of the child, the precious child! The poems and quotes are memorable.

Lessons and insight are on every page. Consider this: "We must prepare ourselves, as an essential part of the environment, in a thousand small ways. We must exist as though the child is always watching, because the child is always watching. The most important lessons we teach are sometimes the ones we didn't know we were teaching.

Everyone I know tells me that life is too busy, too fast. We all have too much to do. Distraction is all around us. Here, we are following the child. Slowly, softly, we watch and listen, as the child moves forward to the next place of readiness. Maria Montessori was a wise scientist and teacher. The Tendencies of Man, so beautifully researched and explained in relationship to the Prepared Environment by Catherine McTamaney, has been transformed by her into a Buddhist-like reflection of our lives and practice as teachers and as humans.

Marie M. Dugan is the former President of the American Montessori Society, where she served as a member of the Board of Directors for over a decade. Her commitment to peace and social justice is evident in her life's work, including her service as an AMS representative to the United Nations. Marie was the founding Chair of the Heads Section of the AMS Board and has chaired the Archives Committee and the Centennial Campaign Commitee. In 2009, she was honored as a "Living Legacy" for the Society. Her lifelong contributions to Montessori and children's education as a teacher, teacher educator and Montessori leader have influenced innumerable lives around the world.

To stimulate life, leaving it then free to develop, to unfold, herein lies the first task of the educator. In such a delicate task, a great art must suggest the moment, and limit the intervention, in order that we shall arouse no perturbation, cause no deviation, but rather that we shall help the soul which is coming into the fullness of life, and which shall live from its own forces. This art must accompany the scientific method.

When the teacher shall have touched, in this way, soul for soul, each one of her pupils, awakening and inspiring the life within them as if she were an invisible spirit, she will then possess each soul, and a sign, a single word from her shall suffice; for each one will feel her in a living and vital way, will recognize her and will listen to her. There will come a day when the directress herself shall be filled with wonder to see that all the children obey her with gentleness and affection, not only ready, but intent, at a sign from her. They will look toward her who has made them live, and will hope and desire to receive from her, new life.

Maria Montessori

The Montessori Method, 1912

Table of Contents

Navigation: An Introduction

Maria Montessori, (1870-1952), anthropologist, educator, and humanitarian, left a far greater legacy than the teaching model that bears her name. Montessori was coming to the end of her life's work when she began discussing the *Tendencies of Man,* a series of eleven qualities unique to human existence. In Montessori's interpretation, the tendencies explained the link between the prepared environment and the needs of the child: the environment was prepared to meet the distinct qualities of human development.

Ever the scientist, Montessori named them, leaving nothing to chance: Orientation, Order, Exploration, Communication, Activity, Manipulation,Work, Repetition, Precision, Abstraction, and, finally, the culmination of all the others, Perfection. Consider the Montessori prepared environment: it is clearly matched to each tendency. The child is offered materials that orient him to his place in the world, that are well ordered, that allow for his free exploration, that build his capacity to communicate, that allow for his active engagement, that provide real experiences to influence and change, that offer him purposeful work, that protect his innate need to repeat, to develop his skillfulness and precision, that move effortlessly from concrete to abstract, and that allow for the perfect emergence of the natural child.

As the Montessori Method becomes increasingly attractive to education reformers seeking better routes to academic achievement, its coherence as an integrated, complete understanding of human development should remain paramount. The Method works as well as it does because it serves, simultaneously and without force, the needs of the natural development of children. That development is not piecemeal. Neither should be its pedagogical response. Montessori's genius lay in her ability to articulate complex matters of human development in a unified model, one which, it turns out, is fairly simple to enact: prepare an environment well suited to the natural development of the child, then get out of the way.

These essays are my effort to articulate Montessori's coherent model for a new generation of teachers and parents. It is part reflection, part workbook, part mandate. I want to offer my readers some questions to consider and some tools for the answering, with a challenge, from one teacher to another, to apply those answers diligently and across our lives, beyond the boundaries of our classrooms or the limits of our teaching. Montessori's Method was not limited to the physical boundaries of our schools. Our practice, as Montessorians, cannot be either.

Each tendency is addressed in its own chapter. Each chapter, in turn, is organized into four parts.

In the first, I offer some questions for conversation. While I understand how challenging it can be to find common ground between people who believe as passionately in their calling as many Montessorians do, I do not believe our teaching is strengthened in isolation. The questions at the beginning of each chapter are designed for our common conversation, as safe prompts from which we may begin to share with each other what has brought us to this practice.

Those initial questions are followed by The Naming of Things, essays specifically written to define the tendency in general, universal ways. I want to begin with a shared understanding of these concepts, particularly as some of Montessori's nuances can be easily lost in translation.

Next, each chapter includes three application essays: The Tendency and The Child, The Tendency and The Self, and The Tendency and Each Other. My hope is that these offer some compassionate reflections on the tendencies as living, relevant and immediate qualities of our lives, informing our practice with children, our challenges as individuals and our potential conflicts with other adults.

Each of the application essays ends with an intention. Maybe you'd call them prayers. Maybe they're poems. Mostly they're thoughts out-loud, hopes articulated from one struggle that I think may be more common than not. They are handwritten, to slow the reader down, to create some intimacy in the writing and in the reading. They're metaphorical notes left pinned to trees in the woods. Someone else has been on this path. Maybe they've left these on their way into the woods. Maybe on the way out. Maybe this is as far as they got. But there are other people on this path. There's plenty of empty space in each chapter. Maybe you'll leave some notes of your own.

There are, despite the loneliness of our classrooms and the heartache of having been called to teach, others on the path with us. Teaching is hard. Teaching in a Montessori path is even more so. Montessorians are asked to give up so much of ourselves, to make ourselves humble and lowly before the child, to be servants, to be scientists, to be saints. We often let ourselves down. There it is, then. We will let ourselves down. But there are others on the path with us. We can lean on each other. We can walk in each other's footsteps. Sometimes we're at the front of the path. Sometimes we're following another traveler. Sometimes we're resting. Sometimes the laughter of our group is so cacophonous that we forget how tired our feet are. Sometimes we're so far ahead or behind that we can't even see each other anymore. But we're not alone.

We are each other's navigational stars. Montessori's words, across generations, guide us. Our own words, whispered in each other's ears or passed in notes or published in books, they give us guidance, too. They remind us on the hardest days that we're not alone. We are not alone. We share certain tendencies, certain traits, common among humanity, common across decades. We are working in common toward a perfection we may never individually see. But we're on the path. And we're not alone.

Namaste.

Orientation

"The child is both a hope and a promise for mankind."

—Maria Montessori

When did you know you wanted to be a teacher?

Has it been since childhood, when some warm smile greeted you to your first day at school, or when you connected with that one voice who made more sense than all the others?

Did you line up teddy bears and baby dolls into your own classroom, or did you hear the call to teach when you lacked the ones you needed yourself? Who were the teachers who touched your soul?

Who guided you to teaching?

When you imagine yourself as Teacher, whose voice do you hear calling in the distance?

I. The Naming of Things

From the Latin, *oriri:* to rise. Orientation is that natural tendency to know where we are and how we fit in with what's around us. The term, "orient," is traced to the early fourteenth century, when it suggested the rising in the east of the sun each morning. In the mid-eighteenth century, it came to mean, "to take one's bearings," or, literally, "to face the east," as the Earth seems to do each morning. When we orient ourselves, we take our own bearings. We search for our physical place and, equally importantly, our spiritual place in the communities we share.

Our desire to understand our physical place is easy to grasp. When we enter a new environment, we look around. How tall is the room? Where is the light? Where will I go once I cross the threshold? Am I comfortable here? What is here that I recognize? North, south, east, west, downtown, uptown, midtown, near the library, across from the school, out back, by the window. We place immediate markers in our minds, and in doing so, we understand our physical place. We know if this is *our* place.

Some of us orient ourselves by the map points: north, south, east or west. Others find our physical place in terms of deeply-engrained knowledge of where things have always been: past McCreavy's auto shop, out by where the post office used to be, not quite to the I-440 intersection. We need to place ourselves within the environment around us, and we do so by situating our place against other objects or benchmarks we presume to be unmoving. Our physical orientation is dependent on our knowledge of what is or was in this space.

Our desire to understand our spiritual place is much more elusive. When we enter a new environment, our spiritual orientation asks different questions. Do I feel comfortable here? Do I know anyone here? Is it what I expected? Do the people here look welcoming? Do I feel at ease? Warm, welcoming, friendly, intimidating, cold, off-putting. . . we place different markers in our mind, with the same hope to understand how we fit in. We place ourselves spiritually within the environment around us, and we do so by situating our place against other places that evoked a similar feeling. This reminds me of home. Industrial architecture feels cold to me. I cannot see around that corner. Our spiritual orientation is dependent on how we feel in this space, on the emotions of comfort and safety or fear and vulnerability the space offers to us.

The need to orient ourselves, both physically and spiritually, is no new phenomenon. Orientation influences rituals across cultures and religious traditions, from the east-west orientation of the world's great cathedrals, to the mandate to face Mecca in Muslim prayer, to the orientation of the angel Morini on Mormon temples or the offering of Native American prayers to the four compass points. From the ancient Mayan cities built from east to west to modern yogis facing east to complete their sun salutations, our spirits seek orientation, that connection to what else is around us, what has been and what is unchanging, to something as profound as the rotation of the Earth or to something as mundane as the closest fire exit. We are driven by an essential human tendency to find our place.

II. Orientation and The Child

Teaching is a calling. We are called to the profession, and we are called each day to the horizon that we cannot see. Our orientation as teachers needs always to point beyond the edge of the map. And although we seek security by understanding where we begin, we do so with an eye on the unknown. We want to know where we are, to know better where we are going.

The children, too, seek their own orientation. For the children in our classrooms, we provide the map points. We offer the careful grids of reliable, thoughtfully placed materials. We offer the same lesson in the same way throughout the year. The terrain is unchanged. Because our classrooms offer a consistent topography, the child can be the cartographer of his own learning, mapping mapping mapping, building his knowledge of the concepts of Practical Life, Sensorial, Math, Language and Culture. As the child readies himself to leave the classroom, his map will have the same hills and valleys as the other children who've discovered alongside him, but the fingerprints will be most assuredly his.

When we are criticized by those who don't understand us, for being too rigid in our routines, too precise in our presentations, we should remind ourselves that the predictability of the Montessori classroom is not for the benefit of some curmudgeonly teacher who just doesn't want the children to be too loud. Our routines are our daily rituals, and like all ritual, they make concrete what may be too big for us otherwise to grasp. They provide landmarks and signposts for the child seeking his own orientation. We tell the child, "You are safe here. Your world is reliable. And your influence here is real."

We admire the harmony of the normalized classroom, when the children have all already found their own paths and are uncovering without our constant guidance. And just as easily, we are frustrated by the rabbit holes and wild geese we run down and chase around, trying to find the pacific. When our guidance for children seems, well, misguided, we return to the basic orientation of the classroom. We look to see what it is in the environment that could be causing the students to stumble. When an alpinist is unable to scale the sheer, glassy face of the mountain, we don't blame the climber. We acknowledge the challenge of the mountain. We look for better tools with which to climb it or an easier path to the top.

Likewise, when the children struggle to orient themselves in the classroom, we look for better tools with which to help them find their way. The child's orientation is clear when he knows his relationship with the environment around him. When that is absent, the child is truly lost. We support the child's orientation by providing reliable, consistent classrooms. The materials, the routines, the presentations remain the same. The terrain does not change. We support the lost child by providing reliable, consistent relationships. We react the same way to the same actions. We welcome the child with the same warmth and acceptance every day. We stand as a constant guidepost. When we know a child is lost, we should never blame the child for his confusion. Instead, we should make more clear the direction we hope he'll follow, and offer a warm welcome down the path.

Today, may I observe the terrain with new eyes

When the child stumbles, may I clear the path

Without chiding the child for falling

May I see the children's struggles as obstacles to overcome

And may I offer

Tools fit to the task

Paths worth walking

Companionship on the trail

May I remember that, though I guide

I can walk only in my own shoes

I can follow only my own path

The child is his own explorer

The discoveries are his to find

III.   Orientation and The Self

We know what to provide for the child who is struggling to orient himself, but in order to provide it, we need to be ourselves sure of the path. Our own orientation, as adults and especially as teachers, is no less important than the orientation of the children we hope to guide. We need to know where we stand. Toward our own sense of place, we seek outside markers, signals and posts to let us know we are where we think we are. What is my job description? What is my title? Who is my boss? Who is my assistant? They're all signposts, helpful because they give us orientation. They tell us north from south. They give us a sense of belonging, these special names and roles. "Because I am the Lead Teacher, I am this. I am not that." "Because I am the Assistant, I do this. I do not do that."

There is security in these concrete trailmarkers, to be sure. But just as we know that the normalized child doesn't need the teacher any more, neither does the normalized adult need these external signposts. They are helpful to us in the same way that an initial lesson is helpful to the child: they give us a simple place from which to begin, and an unspoken challenge to move beyond. When our adult communities are normalized, teachers do what teachers do because that's what teachers do, not because it is in their job descriptions or because their contracts demand it. We hear our calling and we follow it. We feel secure. We don't jump at shadows because we know nothing is lurking around that corner.

It's a long way, though, from relying on the signposts to knowing the way by heart. The path is not clear. And it shouldn't be. Each new community of children is different, even though the terrain remains the same. Likewise, each community of teachers is different, even though the silly job descriptions remain the same. When we rely on our titles and positions to orient ourselves, we remain focused on where we are instead of where we aim to go. We move toward normalization as adults when we acknowledge the goal. When we ask ourselves, "how would I behave if I was already sure of myself here," we shine a light down the path. . . we begin to see ourselves as we wish to become, and we begin to step toward there.

If we are to guide children toward a horizon we cannot see, we need to believe in it ourselves. We need to believe ourselves as capable of the same growth and change and self-direction as we are so certain exists in the child. When we behave without reliance to those signposts, we do what needs to be done, simply because it needs to be done. We take action to move our communities closer toward where we want to be, usually in small steps and sometimes in great leaps. We offer each other help. We share our knowledge and skills. We see ourselves as the teachers we hope to become, we act as though we already are and, in doing so, we magically find ourselves transforming.

May I remember who I wanted to be

When I was called to be a Teacher

May I suspend my fear of the unknown

May I ask for answers

May I ask for help

May I do what needs to be done

When it needs to be done

Because it needs to be done

May I remember the hope

The confidence

The clarity of my calling

And when that call is distant

And the path unclear

When my confidence wavers

And I lose step

May I resist the urge to run along the rocky path Let me slow down

Let me move with caution

Small steps careful steps

Let my work be my guide

IV.   Orientation and Each Other

When we behave as though we are already the teachers we hope to become, we also find ourselves better equipped to offer the same to others. In our need to orient ourselves, we too often fall into habits of territory and self-protection. Feeling unsure of our place, we carve out small worlds of our own divinity. We build walls at the borders.

Where are the borders of your country? Are they at the door of your classroom? Are they in your assertion of your training? Or your presentation of some prized piece of material? What are the parts about who you are as a teacher that are non-negotiable?

Once you've defined them, named them in the map key of your teaching, you need to decide why they're there. Are they an essential part of your teaching, core to what you believe, essential like the ground water? Or are they man-made, built up because that's how you were trained, or because you've never done it a different way? We all have both types: those landforms that are a part of who we are and those which are built up on the surface. The ones we know to be essential help to orient us more clearly. We find, as we identify them, that they cross boundaries. The core parts of our teaching are often the ones that other teachers share, like rivers flowing between countries. We are stewards of those rivers, challenged to keep them flowing, preserving their nourishment. They connect us. We rely on each other through the water we share.

The ones that are inauthentic provide us only temporary shelter. We feel safe behind them, but they keep us from strengthening our practice by keeping us from the other teachers with whom we might grow. An appealing fallacy, but a fallacy nonetheless. They make us bellicose. They are the pedagogical equivalent of land mines, our intellectual weapons that we fire at each other in an effort to protect our own borders. They separate us from each other, and from becoming the teachers we hope to be. How many times have you had a difference of opinion with another teacher, on how to present a material, or what was causing a child's behavior, or what steps to take next, and found that rather than influence your decision, it changed how you felt about that teacher? These conflicts arise when we are unsure of why we believe what we believe. We need not only to name our values, but to understand why they are our values. When we bicker over how we've always done things, we blind ourselves from who we may become.

Some pieces of our teaching are, indeed, so core to who we are and how we've been called that they cannot be discarded. But most of what we do is far more pedestrian, the remnants of our training or the routines that we adopted from previous experience. We can tell the difference by asking, "Why do I believe this dearly? Could I still be the teacher I want to be if I couldn't believe this anymore?" When we start by naming the parts of our teaching we cannot do without, and the ones we could discard, we are better able to build bridges to other teachers, to parents, and, most essentially, to the children. When we start by naming the parts of ourselves we cannot do without, and the ones we could discard, we are better prepared to step off the path and discover something new.

I look to a distant landscape

To a future I cannot see

My teaching is an act of faith in that unseen horizon

That the work I do today

Will help the child tomorrow

And tomorrow

And tomorrow

That the child I nurture today

Will reach that horizon

Will discover new lands

Will blaze trails beyond my ability to imagine

May I provide for him what he needs most on that
adventure

May I not burden him

Or load him down with what we should both discard

Though I cannot see it

Though I'll never see it

May I protect that horizon

Sending it only the seeds of our healthiest blossoms

Trusting the child to reach

To discover

To blaze

Beyond my ability to imagine

Order

"The observation of the way in which the children pass from the first disordered movements to those which are spontaneous and ordered -- this is the book of the teacher; this is the book which must inspire her actions."

- Maria Montessori

Why do they say that Order is Heaven's First Law?

Can you remember a time when you felt confused?

When things weren't happening the way you expected them to or the way you thought they should?

How does confusion feel? What are the other emotions that accompany confusion?

How do you know what to expect, when you know what to expect? When you don't?

How does knowing how things will unfold feel?

What are the other emotions that surround that feeling?

How does order make us more perfect as Teachers?

I. The Naming of Things: Order

We all have a preferred way of doing things, from what side of the bed we like to sleep on to whether we sit down or bend over to put on our shoes. Whether it's where you put your keys or how deep your laundry basket can grow before you absolutely must address it. . . our little preferences, our quirks, the way we like things just because we like them that way: that's our tendency to order.

If you find yourself noticing that all the pencils in the tray are the same length, or straightening a picture that's shifted out of place, that's order. When we notice patterns, or create them, we are seeking order. When we place all the mugs together in the cupboard and all the glasses in their own group, we are creating order. Our need for order infuses our lives, even our messiest, most slovenly friends, even our teenage kids and sloppy roommates. . . look closely enough and you'll find the order there. It might not be your way of ordering things, but it will be there.

This tendency to order emerges early in our lives. For example, own natural rhythms and patterns of sleeping or eating, established even before we are born, reflect our tendency toward order. There is a sense of control in what we can predict.

The first thing we do when we see something new is to decide where it fits with something we know, something we are comfortable with. We try to put it in… order. When our scientists create ever-expanding tables and charts to describe the relationships of everything from galaxies to subatomic particles, they are following the tradition of a thousand generations of humankind.

Imagine the earliest civilizations, trying to understand the arc of sparkles in the night sky. Lacking the scientific evidence to explain the stars, they were no less anxious to understand them. In naming the constellations and developing the stories to explain them, those early civilizations ordered the sky. It is not the available science, but the absence of answers that leads our tendency to name, classify and relate.

Even young children will hold on to plausible, if scientifically unfounded, explanations for how the world works, because those explanations give order to a world which can otherwise be a pretty scary place.

Essentially, it is this fear that propels our internal drive toward order. Order allows for the predictable, and when there is so much which is beyond our ability to predict, the little we can helps to protect us from the immeasurable we can't. Some of these efforts are in the small things, the routines that help get us through the day-- by knowing where I keep my wallet, I am sure to avoid the last-minute-panic to leave the house on time. But some of them are in the universal questions, the ways we define what is human and what is divine, and where in that order of things we place ourselves.

Because, after all, it is not only the external world that we are ordering. We create order to understand our immediate environment, and to place it within the much more important environment beyond our reach. We want to know where we fall in the hierarchy of the universe, whether we define that hierarchy with divinities and seraphim or galaxies and quarks.

II. Order and The Child

We are told in our earliest teacher education experiences, "Children need order." We read it in parenting magazines. Our mothers tell us when our children are born. Our school directors tell us when we are setting up our first classroom. "Children need order."

And so, to the best of our ability, we try to provide it for them. We stand in the same place every morning to shake hands and say hello. We offer each lesson exactly the same way, each movement practiced, from approaching the shelf to inviting the child to work independently. We call the children to lunch at the same time, and have the same routines for going outdoors, and back in again, for arriving and leaving and eating and blowing noses and using the bathroom. We offer the children order through routine. We offer them predictable ways of predictable things happening.

Because children are learning whether the world is a place in which they can trust, we prioritize order, routine and predictability in preparing our environments.

External order, then, leads to internal order. As the child is making sense of the world around her, the more predictable her external environment is, the more coherent that sense-making becomes. As an infant, she begins to connect particular sounds to particular objects. Sounds become words. Words become labels. Labels define objects, or emotions, or relationships. And so the child's internal order is constructed.

Imagine, though, if each time that baby cried, "Dadada," adults around her gave her something different to soothe her. Those sounds would come to mean something else to the infant. They would not develop into "Daddy." Instead, maybe they would mean "I want," or "Soothe me," or "I am sad." Because the external environment reinforces particular ways of ordering the world, the internal environment comes to adopt that same ordering.

Our efforts to provide this order for the child are well-intended. But sometimes, in thinking of the routine we are trying to establish, we overlook the order the child already carries with him. We chide the child for his misbehavior, when his behavior is more hunger than mischief. We bring the child to stimulating environments, filled with new sounds and smells and people, then tell him to sit still. We forget that, just as external order leads to internal order, the child's internal predictions affect how he responds to the external environment.

In Greek mythology, "Chaos" is what comes first, the first created being out of which all the rest of the universe is derived. Good and bad, night and day, Titan and Mother Earth, everything traces its history back to the void. The same is true for children, who can emerge from the chaos of not-knowing to fulfill countless possibilities. Even the youngest children come to us with some sense of how the world should work, limited though it may be. When we disrupt that sense, even if we are disrupting it for good intent, we should not be surprised that the child responds chaotically.

Although all children are moving from chaos to order, the speed, the precision and the trajectory of that movement is as individual as each child.

As we work to create order, through the careful adherence to the routines we want to instill, we must do so with deep compassion for the confusion and disorder the child suffers in the meantime. Lacking the language, the self-restraint and the control that repeated, predictable experiences in orderly environments provides, the child suffers no less deeply for the chaos. He just has fewer words with which to name it. There is order coming from the darkness, though, and it falls to the adult to carry the torch in the meantime.

Little one

Filled with an immeasurable chaos

May I see your struggle for what it is Against what it is

Yearning to know

To predict

To understand

You push to fill the void of unknowing

And I sometimes get in the way

May I offer you

A Name

A Label

A Definition for

Your Way of Knowing

May my work be a torchlight for you

May I offer surety

Calm in the chaos

Clarity in the confusion

May the order I provide grant you Comfort

Assurance

and

Peace

III.   Order and The Self

Each of us has our routines, our little rituals, that give us a sense of order in our classrooms. From what time we enter the room to the perch from which we prefer to observe, we all have our ways of doing things. And remember those days when our order is disrupted, when we are running late or our colleagues interrupt us at an inopportune time, when an unexpected parent conversation becomes more complicated than we expected it to, or the toilet overflows during nap time.

When our carefully ordered environments are thrown into disarray, we often find ourselves feeling like we, too, are airborne, falling without a net.

How do you respond to those days, when nothing seems to be going as planned? Do you add to the chaos with a kinetic urgency? Do you lose your cool, as though by creating more noise you might find your way back to quiet? When our environments are disordered, we often make them even more so by trying to solve all the problems at once. Our teacherly need for control overpowers our better instincts, and we move quickly into crisis mode.

After all, if we didn't think of ourselves as the kind of people who could lead communities of dozens of other people all at once, we wouldn't have found ourselves in the classroom. But you won't decrease the chaos by adding more crisis to it. You can't calm an anxious parent by raising your voice. When the environment seems explosive, it's up to us to defuse it.

We need to remember: chaos is a void. It's not the opposite of order. It's the lack of order. We can't negate it, because it is already an absence. We can only fill it, with quiet, with calm, with order.

Perhaps the best example of this is in that daily test of our patience: false fatigue. When you feel it rising in the classroom, when children are wandering through the space or flopping on the floors, when voices are getting louder and you can hear the pitcher of rice crash in the kitchen, what do you do? Do you quickly ring the bell and get the children to the playground to run off their pent up energy? Do you call them to circle and lead them through "Head, Shoulders, Knees and Toes?"

Or do you find a seat, quiet, calm and orderly, and let the order of the environment reemerge?

When we are tempted to intervene, it is because our own need for order is taking precedence over the internal order we need to trust in the child. And if we were alone in the environment, that might be just fine. You can choose to be as picky as you want about how things are done in your own space, but *your* classroom is not really *your* classroom after all. You are there in service to a different order, and your place is a bit lower on the ranking.

While your internal rhythm may be screaming, "Too loud! Too busy! Too chaotic!" the children are making sense of the chaos. You cannot do that work for them. You can only offer them the model of your own orderly self as an example of how they might respond. And respond they will. That internal order will emerge again, if you give it the space to do so. Without your powerful hand on the reins, the children can take the lead. You have to trust it to happen.

Then watch. Just watch. It will happen.

There is so much

Beyond my control

Beyond my authority

Beyond my influence

Help me to release that which is not mine to hold

Remind me: the children are not mine to hold

Reassure me when I cling

I cling because I am afraid

May I release my fear

May I create order in myself

May I support order in the environment

May I trust the order in the child

Beyond my control

Beyond my authority

Beyond my influence

May I model order within

Compassion without

Courage together

IV.   Order and Each Other

Sometimes the most challenging obstacles we face in our classrooms are not the dozens of children moving in opposite directions, but the single other adult who is supposed to be moving alongside us. This shouldn't be such a surprise. Teachers in the same classroom are often like two drivers trying to steer the same car. It's going to take a lot of coordination if they both want their hands on the wheel. Control that, and the combination will succeed rather than confound.

Think back, though, to what it is that drives our tendency to order. Of all the motivations that propel us, the need for order is the one most closely tied to our need for control. Your need for control is no more important, no more essential, than anyone else's. It's just that your needs and those of the other adults around you are often in conflict with each other.

Which debates draw the most of your energy? Are you frustrated more by the vast gaps in practice across our community or by the colleague in your classroom who calls across the classroom when you would prefer she speak more softly? It's much easier to walk away from the philosophical disagreement you have with a teacher in a different classroom than it is to be patient with the chronically late teacher you have in your own.

But issues of philosophy are much bigger issues! And disagreements there are likely to affect children exponentially, as many times as there are classrooms with teachers with whom we disagree! Why are we so much more comfortable discarding those conflicts than we are with the smaller disruptions of personalities in our own classrooms?

Simple. Our need for control is satisfied by our immediate environment. We feel the arguably unimportant disruption in that environment far more fiercely than the theoretical disagreement with an environment that doesn't affect us personally. And so we focus on the five or ten irritating minutes that our colleague arrives late to our shared classroom instead of the debates of practice that separate us from other teachers. How does it help? We get frustrated with the people with whom we spend the most time while we are accepting and tolerant of the teachers we see only rarely.

And if you are the one who's late? Ah, then, that's the easier problem to solve, isn't it?

Perhaps our efforts, both immediate and universal, would be better served by helping our entire community to move toward better practice. Instead of pointing fingers and distancing ourselves from the people with whom we disagree, what if we took the time to find out what we had in common?

At what level of practice do we agree? If it is not at the level of presentation- in other words, if we disagree about how to show one material or another- maybe we agree at the level of design- that is, what the material is designed to do. If we can't agree at the level of design, maybe we agree at the level of need- what developmental need the material should meet. If we can't agree at the level of need, maybe we can agree on the underlying presumptions of the general method- that children's development is strengthened by the availability of carefully chosen didactic materials in an environment prepared for the child.

We hold more tightly to the *hows* of practice when we are unsure about whether we agree on the *whys*. If we work back to what we believe in common, we can better collaborate on how those common beliefs inform our practice. The same is true whether the debate is about timeliness or the test tubes. In disagreements immediate and small or universal and essential, we are more likely to find resolution to our differences by first finding what we share in common.

In my need for order

For definition and control

In my need for predictability

For routine and reliability

I can lose sight of the forest for the trees

When I forget that what I do is an expression of what I value

May I remember what I value

May I satisfy my need for order

By looking for it first in myself

Am I modeling what I want to become?

Am I offering the compassion I hope will be offered to me?

May I keep my touch

May I keep my focus

May I appreciate both what is unique about each tree

And what is shared among the forest

When my path seems so different than yours

Remind me that we are walking in the same direction

We'll meet in the clearing

Celebrate in the clearing

Exploration

"The senses, being explorers of the world, open the way to knowledge."

- Maria Montessori

What inspires my wonder?

What catches my eye and captures my attention?

When my day is filled with things to do

Tasks to attend to

Have-to's to have-to

What stops me in my tracks and demands my notice?

What don't I know?

I. The Naming of Things: Exploration

The child is an explorer from his first breath, squirming, reaching for warmth, searching for food. He is seeking, so curious about his environment, so curious about sounds, smells, tastes. Even before he can see clearly, he is looking. He is looking for something. This is the soul of exploration, that internal drive to pull back the curtain, to cast light upon shadows, to look around the corner simply because there is a corner there. The theme is repeated, throughout the life of the individual and throughout all of human existence. What we don't know, we want to know. We have to know. It is the essence of the human spirit.

Think about a film or a story that has moved you. How did it describe the human need to explore? Holden Caulfield explores the borders between adolescence and adulthood, in the physical territory of a city that offers him both. Scout Finch explores the limits of faith and goodness as she discovers that her small town answers are not so simple. We want to know about the courage of the men with *The Right Stuff* and the possibilities challenged by the *Little Women* and even the puppies who are *Homeward Bound*. From Dorothy's Adventures in Oz to Ariel's first steps on (what do you call them?) feet? We present protagonists who explore, who go beyond what is known, who map new territories, and we mirror our real-life-tendency toward the same pursuits, incessantly.

And imagine the dull and predictable human existence we'd endure without this essential curiosity. Imagine how simpler our maps would be if we had been satisfied with "Hic sunt dracones." Here there be dragons. What if we had stopped at the known borders, in fear of the dragons beyond?

Certainly, human development owes a debt to the practical issues: following food, seeking shelter, finding safe refuge. Nomads were nomads for pedestrian reasons: they had to move to survive. But beyond our survival, the quality of human development is guided by our insatiable thirst to explore, the wonder and curiosity that lead us to push beyond what we believed we had the capacity to do, beyond what we believed we had the capacity to know. We want to understand the cosmos as deeply as we understand the landscapes of our own minds. When we find a boundary, physical, emotional, intellectual, we want to push beyond it.

Our wonder is the first step of our exploration. When we see something that catches our attention, the way the crescent moon seems to hang on that purple sky, how the tiny legs of a beetle move across a sidewalk, or how my son's smirk reminds me of my father's. . . these moments that make us stop for a moment, lost in thought as our minds make connections across continents and generations: this, too, is exploration. We see something which is different, something out of place or unexpected, and we want to stop, to look more closely, to understand why that thing is not behaving like all those other things.

Wonder frames the questions our explorations answer. That's what makes wonder such a powerful experience. The questions we are deeply driven to answer insist upon our notice. They catch our eyes and our imaginations and they demand that we look.

Exploration is the insatiable tendency. We may finish our formal education, but we never lose our intrinsic drive to learn. There is no time in our development when we have learned enough, when we know enough, when there are no mysteries left to be solved. Even at the moments of our deaths, we are still wondering, we are still exploring. What will come next? What is beyond the curtain? We begin our lives reaching for what we can't see, and we end them the same way, squirming, reaching, searching, seeking, exploring.

II. Exploration and The Child

The Montessori classroom relies upon the child's natural drive toward exploration. We presume that children's authentic curiosity will show itself to us, and that, by linking the concrete materials with the child's interest, we can elevate learning beyond rote memorization. And once we have demonstrated the material, we anticipate the child will discover for himself its special qualities, its self-correction, its isolated concept. We expect that, even before the child may have the capacity to articulate his discoveries, his exploration will lead to a deep and grounded understanding of every number of concepts.

For even the most best-intended teacher, though, the child's tendency toward exploration can be a frustration. Driven by an internal mandate to understand, the child is incessant in his questioning, in his doubt, and his curiosity. "Why?" the child asks, and when we answer, he asks again, "Why?" Over and over and over again. "Why?"

The child challenges our patience. He challenges our ability to speak clearly, to communicate effectively, to teach masterfully, when he asks, "Why?" Over and over and over again. "Why?" And while our rational selves may understand that his questioning follows the courageous vision of the explorer, the more petty versions of ourselves, hassled and exasperated by the questions we cannot answer, would very much like for the child to just stop asking already. This is the child who demands our humility.

Another child, driven by the tendency toward exploration, demands our own curiosity. This is the child who does not ask anything of us except to be left alone, the child who is so engaged so deeply in the material that his explorations are singularly focused on the work before him. This is the child who discovers qualities of the materials we may not have known ourselves, who spends hours sliding the tiniest cube of the Pink Tower along the ledges of the other nine cubes, the child who lies his head sideways on the table to see how the light shines through the stream of water pouring from pitcher to pitcher. Engrossed in his wonder, he is easily overlooked. He requires us to observe him differently, because he will not demand our attention. In fact, he will resist it.

To understand him, we need to share his wonder. We need to slow down, to quiet down, to settle down, and to observe. Breaking his concentration, stealing his wonder, leaves us both at the deficit. By insisting that he move it along, we keep him from his intrinsic need to explore what is wonder-ful to him. What propelled him will still be there, but he will know not to trust it to us.

Finally, there is the child who demands our patience, the explorer who follows paths we would not have chosen for him, who explores the materials or pushes the boundaries of the classroom or challenges our own boundaries in ways we did not expect and with results we emphatically do not welcome. As explorers ourselves, we should see this child as a puzzle for our own curiosity. If we can explore his motivation, we can discover what drives his behavior. If we can recognize his ability to question the well-traveled paths of our classroom as a quality to elicit our own wonder, we may see him as an inspiring horizon instead of an irritating obstacle.

And that, after all, is the first and always work of the teacher: to see each child as he is yet to be, to look beyond both the forest and the trees to the view from the top of the mountain.

Each of these children reminds us of our place in the expedition. We are not in the classroom to direct the exploration, but rather to carry the equipment and check the supplies. Our work is to scout, to observe, to inform, but ultimately to *follow the child*. Safe travels.

I have traveled these paths before I am anxious to move along

To move them along

The paths before me are the well-worn footprints of earlier expeditions

May I remember that they were once rough terrain

May I follow the child's curiosity

Even when it veers from the path

Especially when it veers from the path

This journey is not measured in speed

But in discovery

One eye

on the horizon

The other

on the mysteries at my feet

III.   Exploration and The Self

As adults, our need for exploration may seem frivolous. We are told to settle down. We have commitments to uphold. We shake our heads at the friends and classmates who still haven't discovered what they want to be when they grow up. We equate maturity with stability, and stability with root-taking. We are wrong on both counts.

Despite our best efforts to grow up, we still look longingly to the horizon. We just limit our searching to summer vacations or once-in-a-lifetime trips, as though our need to explore can be satisfied with a cruise to Alaska or a pilgrimage to see the Egyptian pyramids. There are, indeed, vast and exotic and extreme drives for exploration, but there are also countless different ways we are driven to explore our immediate worlds. That tendency is no less essential. Every time we go to the movies, or we watch television, every time we escape into a book or an online site, we are exploring. What else is escapist entertainment but a means to explore the lives we don't lead? Whether we are imagining ourselves as powerful tycoons or film stars or commending ourselves for not being as miserable as the cast of some reality show, we are putting on another role. We are exploring the world through someone else's experience of it. And in doing so, we understand our own experiences a little differently. I know I am this because I know I am not that.

Thankfully, not all exploration is escapism. Most is just the opposite. Our tendency to explore as adults is equally critical as the child's same drive. We are compelled to understand what we don't already understand, to ask new questions and to seek new answers. Sometimes we do that through public, groundbreaking ways, like the scientific innovations that have so rapidly changed our society. The law of accelerating returns continues to astound.

But mostly, we do it in quiet ways, in internal explorations that help us better understand who we are and why we do what we do. When we take the time to explore our motivations, to cast light upon our personal shadowlands, we make ourselves better able to improve the our society. When we understand why we are who we are, we give ourselves the permission to change, to strengthen those parts of ourselves we want to protect and to cast off what interferes with our momentum. These quiet, personal, private explorations are no less important to our human development. They may not make the headlines, but they have the capacity to change our culture in immeasurable ways.

First, though, we need to acknowledge that we are worthy to make the trip. Who are we to warrant such study? Why does it matter to anyone else why I lose my temper when I do, or how I miscommunicate when I do, or what my biases or prejudices are? Surely, my life is not so unique that it requires deep scrutiny. But when we allow ourselves to explore our intentions, to work back from what irks us or understand why we are attracted to particular things, we are more mindful in our actions. When we take the time to ask challenging questions about ourselves, we turn off the auto-pilot in our lives and turn on real living. We can make vibrant choices. We can experience the world with a deeper gratitude. We can engage with each other, with our communities, with our children, and with ourselves, with understanding, with knowledge and with intent. In order to change our world, first we have to understand it. To understand the world, we must first understand ourselves.

My life is ordinary

Typical

Predictable

I work

I clean

I sleep

I breathe

My life is extraordinary

Unprecedented

Exceptional

I love

I laugh

I embrace

I change

In my ordinary days

May I remember my extraordinary self

My life is more than the work I do

My spirit a rich vast unchartered territory

Worthy of the exploration

IV.   Exploration and Each Other

The distances between us, as teachers, parents, adults who are supposed to be "in charge," are often wide chasms. Einstein had it perfectly right: before you can see the truth of an answer, you must first fix the position of the observer. That position will vary the truth and leave observers to argue the nonexistent contradictions. We may be looking at the same situation, but our individual territory interferes. When we disagree, we see each other across miles of misunderstanding, through the heavy fog of miscommunication. We speak in foreign tongues. We are alien.The truth is still right there. It is only our positions as observers that cause the fog.

And in these moments, do you see yourself as the foreigner or do you cast your colleague into that role? Do you accept without question the correctness of your own observation and dispute the validity of any other? We understand our own perspective, and so often we find some deficit in the "other" who cannot see the world through our eyes, the "alien" whose own life has instilled different norms, different ways of being, different languages, contrary observations.

If ever there were a time for curiosity, it is when two people don't get along. If we can receive each "other" with a curious spirit, if we can see each "other" as a new land to explore, we may find the firm walls between us crumbling down.

Imagine this: you and I disagree. We disagree vehemently. We disagree passionately. And we disagree about something that is deeply important to both of us. Concession is not an option. I can declare my boundaries, and name you as my enemy, or I can invite you to explore our borders together.

To explore can mean to traverse, as in the great distances of a countryside, or to scrutinize, as in the tiny differences between us. Explore finds its root in the Latin, "to cry out," a reference to the hunting cries that connected us in the wilderness. When we are at odds, it is like we are lost in the dense woods. . . what better time to cry out to each other? Where are you? I am here.

Our tendency for exploration is then the natural balance to our tendency toward orientation. Just as we want to know where we are in the universe, and how we relate to each other, we are driven to seek each other out when we are lost. While our need for orientation makes firm our stance, our tendency to explore can give us the courage to take a step closer to each other.

Approaching each other with curiosity, in times of distress or, even more importantly, in everyday situations, strengthens our bonds. We are allies instead of adversaries.

When we see each other as deserving of our curiosity, we ask interesting questions, we listen more attentively, and we are able to see each other as richer, more vibrant, more wonder-ful travelers. We discover this in each other when we explore without expectation, driven purely by our curiosity, our belief that what we don't know is deserving of our wonder.

Lao Tzu said, " A good traveler has no plans and is not intent on arriving." We must explore each other as good travelers, leaving behind our trappings of what you should believe or how I should act, greeting each other instead with the same awe and admiration as if we were encountering one of the Great Wonders of the World. Because, truly, that's what each of us is, if we dare to look closely enough. We are each a great wonder, an unknown territory worthy of exploration and deserving of the trip. There is yet another corner. You are around that corner. We call out to each other, *"Where are you? I am here."*

Who are you?

Are you friend or foe?

Are we traveling in the same direction

Or threatening each other's borders?

When we disagree, we stand apart

We can squint at each other across the canyon

Or we can climb down from our perch

To the common land between us

When you are a stranger,

May I greet you as divine.

May I welcome you with Curiosity

Fascination

Wonder

May I remember that the view is just as Curious

Fascinating

Wonderful

From where you are

Communication

"The child has other powers than ours, and the creation he achieves is no small one; it is everything."

- Maria Montessori

"Let thy words be counted."

What is worth saying?

What do I hear? What are the messages I choose to attend to?

Which ones would I rather throw away?

How do I make myself heard?

What do I share?

I. The Naming of Things: Communication

From the moment of our births, we are calling out to each other. Our need to communicate is essential to our humanness, that drive to connect to other people, across generations or across a room, to read each other's eyes, to hear each other's voices, and to know that we, too, are heard. Before we have words, we understand how to communicate. As infants, we cry out. We reach. We pull and hold tight to what we need. We toss aside what is useless to us. Even without words, we connect with our eyes, attending to faces, mirroring expressions, connecting and communicating.

Indeed, the drive is so intense that the ability to communicate serves as one of the most critical benchmarks in our lives. We track when our children speak their first words, when they connect two words together, when they are able to answer questions or speak in full sentences. Long before we think of "teaching" the child, she is compelled to learn to communicate. Within a year, she has adopted the norms of her native tongue. Within two, she is able to manipulate those rules to express herself. Within three, she is able not only to understand the exceptions, but to use a complicated and expansive vocabulary to engage in limitless ways.

The drive doesn't decrease with the mastery of spoken or written language, though. Throughout our lives, we seek ways to communicate to each other. We learn to read body language. We can convey a million thoughts with a single arched eyebrow. We rely on our ability to communicate for practical issues, but just as importantly, we manipulate it to understand more deeply the world around us. We communicate to hear and to be heard.

Beyond the limits of our individual lives, the means by which we communicate mark the development of humankind. When we study ancient cultures, we look for evidence of communication. Did they use pictures or letters to write? How did they convey their values? What did they document and what did they disregard? In more recent history, we know our modern civilizations are paced by an ever-increasing speed of communication. From the critical invention of the printing press, we have sought ways to communicate with more people, across farther distances, in shorter time. Technology allows us to see around the world without delay, and we look. Limited by methods that rely only on our voices, we develop technologies to send our images simultaneously. Our youngest generation, dissatisfied with the near instantaneous speed of mobile communication, abbreviates our language to be able to share their ideas with fewer keystrokes.

Indeed, our need to communicate is inherent to who we are as a species, across our lifetimes and across the millennia of human existence. If we are unable to use our voices, we use our bodies. If we are unable to use our bodies, we use our eyes. We record our first words and our last ones. We are driven to connect to each other, and to do so, whenever possible and despite earth-spanning distances, as though we were in the same room. When we communicate, we share ourselves. We imprint the world with our perspective. Insistently, we call out to each other, "Hear me. I will listen."

II. Communication and The Child

Montessori classrooms are sometimes criticized for being too quiet, too orderly, too "adult" in their environments, as though a quiet community of children is an unnatural one. In healthy Montessori classrooms, though, the quiet is not a result of adult insistence, but of children's attentiveness, of their focus on the work that drives them and of their ability to communicate with each other in meaningful ways. Children who feel heard do not need to yell. Children who have the tools to convey complex messages do not oversimplify.

Children do need to communicate, to share, to impart. Like adults, children enter into fellowship when they communicate. They give to something beyond themselves. They make their whole greater than the sum of their parts. Allowing free communication, then, is an essential part of the classroom experience. If we believe Montessori classrooms should be places in which children's natural tendencies are respected, we must allow for open communication.

Why, then are some of the most productive Montessori classrooms the quietest? Simple. Communication is not the same thing as noise. Communication isn't chaotic. Communication isn't unbounded. True communication involves multiple people, sharing, imparting, joining in fellowship with each other. True communication involves intentional messages. True communication is subtle. It's nuanced, and it's often quiet. We should not mistake the calm of a busy Montessori classroom for a lack of communication. Every time a child stops to watch another child's work more carefully, there is communication. When two children work together, following each other's cues, solving problems simultaneously, there is communication. When one child notices that another is sad, and offers the peaceful comfort of his or her company, there is communication. This is authentic communication: an idea is conveyed, received and responded to.

Further, while often communication serves our basic functions, like all human development it evolves past the practical and toward the sublime. That evolution, from calling out when we are hungry to sharing our more reflective observations of our communities, requires the ability to use rich language in subtle ways, to convey increasingly complicated messages. Montessori classrooms offer children these tools. The verbal and written language of the classroom is accurate, often scientifically so. Teachers design their messages to be precise and clear. Words and actions are intentional. These environments model thoughtful communication and they trust that, given the right opportunities, children are capable of the same.

Essential to the task, then, is the deep respect for children's developing ability to communicate. Listening carefully, giving children ample time to articulate their thoughts, asking thoughtful, probing questions, modeling high-quality language and offering it when a child is frustrated… our classrooms can allow the opportunity for children's communication to evolve beyond the narrow presumptions many adults make. By offering the child the tools to express his most complicated observations, we offer the child an opportunity to share with us more than his message. We offer the child to opportunity to share himself.

Let my mind be open

And my mouth closed

Remind me

The limits of the child's vocabulary

Are not the limits of the child

She has something to say

Let me give her words when she needs them

Let me help her to name her world

She has something to say

Let me put aside my own message

And instead help her to find her own voice

She has something to say

Listen

She has something to say

III.   Communication and The Self

Because the need to communicate is so essential to our human development, and because it requires the attention and involvement of at least one other person, it is perhaps the most difficult for the teacher in the classroom to balance with her responsibilities to the children. Our professional obligation, after all, is not to the message we want to convey, but to the creation of an environment within which the children's development comes first. It is impossible to hear the messages the children are sending if we don't first stop talking. And yet, our own drive to communicate often gets in the way of our self-restraint. We mistakenly believe that we can find the right words to teach, forgetting that the child does not learn by our telling, but by his action.

In the overscheduled, overextended cacophony that is most of our lives, it may be hard to view our silence as an essential part of our need to communicate. The drive to communicate, after all, is not just to speak, but to share, to impart ourselves to something outside ourselves. We can't understand how what we've shared has been understood if we don't allow for time for silence. Our silence, as teachers, is our opportunity to observe, to hear more purely the messages the children are sending so that we can respond to them rightly.

This is especially important in the classroom, when our communication should be limited to those precise efforts to prepare the environment within which children can thrive unobstructed by our agenda. When we are in the classroom, we have a single message to convey: this world is yours. Explore.

We communicate that message not by correcting, or lecturing, or redirecting over and over and over again, but, often and most powerfully, without words, through the example of the lessons we offer and the model of our own behavior in the classroom. When the community fails to emerge as we would hope, or when a child challenges us in an unpredictable way, we struggle to say the right thing. We look for the right words to put things back on track. We won't find them. Just as the children communicate through their attention, through their nurture, their choices and their action, so must we if we are going to speak their language. Put aside your words. Consider instead your actions. What are you attentive to? What do you nurture, and what do you ignore? What do you do and what does that action communicate? It is not the children's responsibility to hear you. It is your responsibility to hear them, to understand them, to translate their actions into an appreciation for their needs, their drives and their motivations, and to design the environment which fulfills them.

This communication requires a great humility, a willingness to observe and to respond instead of to direct and to control. It's backstage, not center stage. But the message it conveys is critical, not only to our teaching today, but to humanity tomorrow: The child deserves to be heard. It is an act of faith, that a generation of listened-to children may become adults who don't need so much to scream.

I will not always like what I hear

I may want to change the message

I may want my words to be yours

When what I am trying to say seems to fall on deaf ears

May I say less and listen more

I promise to listen

I promise to hear you

I will be your voice

When I speak on behalf of the child

Help me to first put aside my adult distortions

Help me to put aside my agenda

Help me to put aside the grammar of my own intentions

When I speak as an advocate of the child

I speak as the voice of the future

To be your voice, I promise first to silence mine

I promise first to hear you

I promise first to listen

IV.   Communication and Each Other

In every interaction with another person, we communicate something... sometimes intentionally so, and sometimes by the happenstance of our context. When we communicate, whether on purpose or by presumption, we share a bit of ourselves with each other. We open ourselves up. We expose our intentions, our values, our hopes, bit by bit by bit.

Perhaps this is why we are so frustrated when we feel unheard, when we are misunderstood. Because we are giving of ourselves when we communicate, we want to be sure that what we give is received truthfully, that it is not eroded in the giving.

What we share is important. It deserves to be understood. And sometimes it's lost in translation. Sometimes life and language gets in the way. So, sometimes, we blame the listener for not hearing. We are frustrated when someone else, "just doesn't get it."

No one can know your heart as well as you do. No one can understand it as completely. No one speaks exactly the same language as anyone else. We are fluent, it's sure, in each other's communication, but we each speak only one native language- that unique combination of context, experience, and meaning that defines our individual lives.

It's no surprise that we are sometimes misunderstood. And an equal miracle when we feel completely heard.

Have you ever felt totally understood? Have you had a friend who you trusted always knew what you were thinking? Someone with whom you connected so easily, so clearly, that you were never aware that you were speaking different languages. These connections happen rarely for most of us. We give them special names. They are our "soulmates." They are "like sisters." If the complicated equation of human interaction has offered you the opportunity: listen.

These are distinct and wonderful opportunities, not only to feel deeply understood, to feel some satisfaction to the human tendency to communicate, to share, to impart, but to push our knowledge of ourselves even deeper. When we find someone with whom we do not need to translate, we can explore the limits of how we define the world. We can challenge ourselves and our presumptions with less threat of mischaracterization. From the safety of our native tongue, we can learn to express ourselves more profoundly. Speak loudly. Speak clearly. Listen.

And because these moments are so rare, so priceless and, often, so irreplaceable, offer yourself and the people with whom you stumble through translation a bit of grace. Because there will be more of those moments, after all. It is more likely that another teacher, or a parent, or a child, will hear our messages through their own native language than through ours. It is more likely that our efforts to communicate will be filtered through our listener's own lens than through ours. Perhaps if we presume less understanding, we will take more care in the way we choose to make our messages known. We might ask less of each other. We might expect more of ourselves. We might choose our words carefully, share ourselves more thoughtfully, leave less to chance. And perhaps we'll be understood more often.

Mine is a language of one
My voice My experiences My life
My definition

What is natural to me
Is foreign to you
What is native to you
Exotic to me

When we misunderstand each other,
Help me to slow down my translation
To hear you more clearly
Understand you with less confusion
To become fluent in you

Help me to slow down my translation
To share with you more clearly
To make myself understood with less confusion
To teach you to be fluent in me

Help me to remember that your need to be understood

matches mine

Your need to be heard

matches mine

Your need to speak

matches mine

The language we share speaks louder than either of us
alone

Activity

"No one can be free unless he is independent: therefore, the first, active manifestations of the child's individual liberty must be so guided that through this activity he may arrive at independence."

- Maria Montessori

Remember what it felt like to be told

Sit still.

Quiet down.

When you were reprimanded for your movement

Remember what it felt like

Tiger in a cage

Dog on a chain

Child in a chair

Is it any easier now?

Or have you just gotten used to the feeling?

I. The Naming of Things: Activity

From before we are born, we are active. We are moving, gliding, pressing out, pushing forward, adjusting our position in space, in time, in relation. Activity is, indeed, that first yelling out, "Here I AM!" What anxious mother doesn't hold her hand pressed to her belly, waiting waiting waiting for the first signs of activity within? What joy and unexpected laughter and exuberance we share when we feel that baby's kick. Before our children can speak, before we hold them or touch them or look into their eyes, before we hear their cries or kiss their faces, we know them because they are *active*. Before we know what they look like, or understand their personalities, or worry for their futures or beam at their accomplishments, we connect with them through their *activity*, through that essential, forceful insistence: "Here I am. I am of you, but I am. I move. I kick. I wiggle. I am."

This need for activity, this innate drive to move, to be in and of our own bodies, leads us from our first journey out of the womb to each new physical discovery and behind. We reach with our bodies and with our minds towards new experiences. Without an active mind we cannot imagine the unseen. Without an active body, we cannot discover it.

Which is not to say that all activity shares direction. Not all activity has a place in mind to go. We are compelled to be active whether or not we have anyplace to be.

Think about those times when an unexpected turn in the weather keeps you inside for days on end, or when your patience is challenged to be still too long, when your mind wanders for a lack of stimulation or your feet shake under the table for a lack of somewhere to go. We still insist on activity, even when we have nothing that needs being done. Activity is not about completing a task. We are active for the sake of being active.

We measure the quality of our lives by the quality of the activity within them. We track brain *activity*. We look for cellular *activity*. We search the rubble for signs of *activity*.

Even at the end of our lives, our caregivers note when we are actively dying, when the efforts of our bodies and our minds collaborate toward their shared close.

In this light, then, perhaps we can be a bit more forgiving of ourselves and of each other when our human insistence on activity interferes with our contrived expectations of stillness. Physical stillness does not demand intellectual stillness, and indeed, is often its worst enemy. How often do we expect ourselves to sit still, to move, engage, think, less, to be passive, when every fiber in our beings calls us to be active. When we know we must be physically passive, how can we nonetheless allow for our intellectual activity? If we must be still, how can we still be active?

We are not called to lead passive lives. To be active is to be alive, even until the moment of our deaths.

II. Activity and The Child

We know children must move. We know their bodies compel them to be active, to engage and to act upon their environment. And so we prepare environments within which they can. We offer them open spaces. We allow them free movement. We invite them to move about, to move the materials, to move their tables, to move their bodies, as, we hope, they learn what we want for them to learn. We give them space to lie down and opportunities to practice carrying heavy things. We invite them to purposeful activity, that perfect balance of physical and intellectual engagement. When it works.

But how often do we reprimand children when their activity contradicts what we would have of them? How often do we chide them to sit still? And how often do we use stillness as a punishment. You have been too active at group time, so now you must go sit alone. You have moved too quickly in our environment, so now you must not move.

Absurd? When else would we respond to the expression of a human need by its further deprivation?

We would not withhold food from a hungry child. We would not punish a child's thirst by insisting he not drink. But we reprimand children's equally essential, inherent need for movement by restricting them to *stillness*. And in doing so, we associate being still with being naughty. We teach children that we would prefer they disengage than interrupt.

Remember the old rule of teacher preparation: we don't correct unintentional error. Surely, there are right times for right action. Surely, it is part of our work as teachers to help children to connect them.

But children's impulses don't reflect their intention: that's what makes them impulses. When a child's movement is because the child cannot not move, what good is punishment? When a child's movement is because the child cannot not move, movement is the only right response.

The child who runs through the classroom? Invite her to carry the goblet without spilling a drop of its precious water.

The child who wiggled incessantly during group? Let him be your reminder that group time has run too long.

When our agendas demand more of the children than the children's development can return, we should correct the *agenda,* and not the child.

Children's activity is inherent, compelling, and for its own wonderment. Children move and dance. They wiggle. They leap sideways and backwards. They squat. They invert. They roll on the floor and climb on the furniture, not because they are going anywhere in particular, but simply because they are going.

And while we might discourage them from bouldering up the antique sideboard, we can nonetheless rejoice in the crazy beauty of their moving bodies. To be so completely, just to be, fully, entirely, embracingly in one's own body, to exalt in the extension of one's fingers, to burst forth from this physical world. . . what life!

So watch the child as she watches herself in the mirror, as she discovers the angles her body makes, as she juts elbows and splays knees, as she dances. She is absorbed by the wonder of her body. To ignore it, to rush it along, to force it to sit still. . . what loss, what complete, thorough, maddening loss. To recapture that wonder for a moment. . . what life! To reconnect to it in ourselves when we observe it in the children. . . what a gift!

Where are you going, that you have to get there so quickly?

Why must you always run?

Why can't you just sit still?

Be where I am.

Be still.

When your activity and my agenda collide,

May I remember that I am your servant, not your shepherd.

May I remember that, wherever it is you're going,

It's my job to follow.

May I remember that where you are right now

Is perfect

Is joyful

Is active

Is alive

That you are as wonderful as your every movement.

That you are as wonder full as your wonderment.

May I receive you as you are

Not as an interruption to my momentum

71

But as a reminder of when I was perfect

Joyful active alive.

May I dance with you

May I be. Still.

III.   Activity and The Self

As adults, we often overlook or undervalue our need for activity. We do our daily tasks. We complete our chores. We take care of what needs to be done. We do so, almost robotically, habitually moving through one task or another. But when are we active?

We watch TV and forget what show we are watching during the commercial. We reread the same passages in our magazines without really taking in what we've read. We skim through or over endless emails, graphics, ads, pictures on screens big and small, ignoring most of what we see. We see endless images. But when are we active?

Is it any wonder that we feel so restless all the time? When are we active?

To be active is to be engaged. To be active is to be connected, to our bodies, to our minds. To be active is to be alive, and when we are not engaged, when we are not connected, we hunger for life. To be active is to be sentient, to be conscious, to be alert, to be attentive. When we are not conscious, when we are not attentive or alert, we hunger for sense.

Our drive for activity compels us to engage, to be fully present in our bodies and our minds.

Activity is not wild movement, unbound or uncontrolled. Activity is engagement, physical and intellectual. It is presence, sentience, life. It is life itself.

Our challenge, then is not to avoid those tasks that we can move through without being active, but to engage them with active minds and active bodies. There are so many have-tos that we simply have-to. Being actively engaged will not, for example, take out the recycling any less often, but it may allow us to do so without abdicating our liveliness in the meantime.

Whatever the task, lofty or banal, we can fulfill with our presence and attention.

And as we seek to engage our intellects, to be more actively present in the every day tasks of our lives, we should not overlook the equally forceful human need to be active in our bodies. Our bodies need to move, just as they did when we were children. Just as we make space for children to work from different positions, to sit sometimes and stand sometimes and sometimes lie down, our bodies demand equal stimulation.

When we move our bodies, we reconnect with the concrete environment. We reconnect the abstract world of our imagination with the real world around us. We make possible what we imagine. We make real what we dream. We understand our limits and how to surpass them. But we cannot identify the boundaries beyond our control if we restrain ourselves the contrived boundaries within our control. If we tell ourselves there is a limited number of ways to work, if we tell ourselves that adults sit at desks, or only move slowly, or do not dance, we limit who we are and what we could become.

Is it any wonder then that we feel so restless all the time?

Our restlessness, physical and intellectual, is our real drive to be active calling out against our contrived insistence to be passive. Listen.

What is it about being grown that demands I be still?

Why I am afraid to dance?

So, someone might see me.

So, someone might laugh.

So, someone might think,

"Look at her. She's not as serious as I thought she was."

So?

Someone might see me.

Someone might laugh.

Someone might think I'm not as serious as I thought I was.

If I have to choose,

May I choose engaged

May I choose sentient

May I choose conscious.

May I be the one laughing.

IV.   Activity and Each Other

Think of a time when you have you felt really heard. How could you tell? Maybe the person you were with held your eye contact. Maybe she asked questions that probed your thinking and telling more deeply. Maybe she offered guidance that understood the subtle complexity of your situation.

Think of a time when you felt overlooked. How could you tell? Maybe the person looked away often. Maybe she responded with simple comments that seemed unconnected to what you had said. Maybe she dismissed what was essential about your message in exchange for what was expedient.

We feel heard when we feel connected, when our companionship is active. We feel overlooked when our interactions are passive.

We feel connected when we are sure that the people we are with are actively with us.

Sometimes that's physical, when we are playing or moving or dancing with another person and we know we are in time with each other. Sometimes it's intellectual, when we are talking or sharing or listening with another person and we know, again, we are in time.

But just like you can step on your dance partner's toes if you're not paying attention, just being in someone's presence does not guarantee your engagement.

Just as you know with whom you will feel heard, you can probably name just as easily with whom you will be overlooked. Sharing space is not the same as sharing ourselves. We can be passive in a crowd.

We hunger for the company of those with whom we feel connected. And we know that, if we are to receive that sustenance, we must offer it ourselves.

A companion, after all, is not just someone with whom you share space. A companion, from the Latin com- and -pan, is someone with whom you share bread, someone with whom you share sustenance, someone whose presence leaves you full. We seek companionship in the same way we seek food or water, as an answer to our hunger. Failing that, we can spend endless hours sharing space with another person and feel disconnected and alone nonetheless.

Active engagement is a crop to be tended, just like any source of sustenance. We need to offer ourselves, actively, to each other, if we are to find the people who will do the same for us.

Active engagement, luckily, like any spiritual bread, is an easy crop to tend. It blossoms with just a bit of care. We find ourselves receiving it in equal proportion to our efforts, and multiply it with ease. We may be able to satisfy our need for an active mind and an active body by ourselves, but we will hunger with our need for active engagement with others unless we plant those seeds ourselves. We must start with ourselves. We must begin by being attentive, being present, being active with others, if we are to harvest from that garden. When a garden fails to fruit, we do not blame the seed. Our connection to each other, that essential, sustaining, active bounty, begins with our own attentions, and we rarely need to look beyond the people with whom we share our vocation to harvest it. Blossom where you are planted.

Some days feel like a famine

Nothing grows here

Nothing blossoms

I am sustained by what makes me conscious

I am sustained by what makes me active

I am sustained by what makes me sentient

When I am surrounded by what is vast and dry and barren

May I find the seed within myself

To listen to you

To connect with you

To engage with you

To be with you

That we may be connected

That we may be engaged

That we may be sentient

Active

That we may share in our harvest

Manipulation

"We then found that individual activity is the one factor that stimulates and produces development, and that this is not more true for the little ones of preschool age than it is for upper school children."

- Maria Montessori

What are the tools you cannot live without?

Do you have a favorite pen?

Your grandfather's hammer?

Your mother's cast-iron skillet?

What meaning is infused with the years of use?

What memories of a world imagined just a bit better?

I. The Naming of Things: Manipulation

We track the evolution of the species by when our ancestors developed tools, knowing that the ability to make use of objects for our own purposes reflects not only a physical change, but a change in our understanding of the world. To manipulate our environment is to exert some control over it, to change the world from what it was when we got there to something better, stronger, different.

In early societies, this need pushed along evolution: controlling fire, constructing tools, harvesting the earth. The organizations of humans reflected the tools available to us, and were moved forward when those tools changed. And those tools did more than just change where we lived or what we ate. They embedded a belief that this earth was something we could control, this environment was something we could master, a sort of cosmic chicken-and-egg. Does our desire to rule the world come from our ability to influence it, or does our drive to develop those means of influence come from our desire to rule the world?

Look for the evidence of our human need to manipulate: it is present everywhere, from world-spinning changes in technologies to the doodles you trace with a stick in the sand. As individuals, we are compelled to influence our environment. As groups, or organizations or larger societies, we mirror this same drive, working together, making as much use of each other as of the tools in our hand.

So much of our current tool-making is in virtual routes- paths to make the transfer of invisible data, the speed of intangible communication, of images and words, that much faster, seamless, immediate. As we dervish in these imaginary exchanges, we need to remember our physical selves. How do you feel after a day in front of the computer, when you have not moved your body, when your only work has been in your mind?

We seek out tools to make our lives more efficient, to capture back more time of a better quality for the activities and people we enjoy. But all too often, we fill up that new found time with more tool making. Our societal evolution may be toward increasingly abstract worlds, but we, nonetheless, remain very much tied to this physical one. Our tendency toward manipulation is not satisfied by screens and displays. We must move. We must act upon real things. We must use real tools that engage our bodies. Whether it is through a garden shovel in our backyards, or an electric drill on a building site, or a golf club on a Sunday afternoon, our bodies and our minds need time when we connect our concrete need to manipulate with the real, physical world around us. This, too, is manipulation, albeit of a far more essential, more satisfying means. So long as we have these bodies, we will have the need to use them. They are the first and most important tools of our minds. Let's not let them rust.

II. Manipulation and The Child

Drop the spoon. Retrieve the spoon. Drop the spoon. Retrieve the spoon. Drop the spoon. Retrieve the spoon. Remember that fantastic, wonderful, infuriating game of infancy? Drop the spoon. Retrieve the spoon. Drop the rattle. Retrieve the rattle. Drop the toy. Retrieve the toy. Remember the frustration of leaning over, again and again and again and again. Pick it up. The baby drops it. Pick it up. The baby drops it. Again and again and again and again.

This wildly infuriating game may seem like infant-driven torture to most caregivers, particularly the ones who are just trying to get some food into the baby's mouth. But for the child, this is the one example of the inherent human need for manipulation. The child is learning the consequences of his actions. What will happen when I. . .? Will it happen again if I do it again? And again? And again and again and again?

The child is a scientist, exploring his world, experimenting with what is reliable and what is unfounded. And like any good scientist, he replicates. When he approaches a conclusion, he tests it. And tests it again. And again and again and again. While his caregivers wish he would just stop dropping the spoon already, that emerging brain is at far more important work than we can see. Retrieving the spoon (or the rattle or the toy or the shoe or the bowl or the. . .) teaches the child that he can influence his world, that his efforts are reliable, his environment secure.

That need to manipulate the environment is essential to the Montessori classroom, where children's ability to influence and act upon and build their space is a key quality of the classroom design. From moving tables at lunchtime to the tiny movements of the tweezers, the Montessori classroom offers children real experiences mastering real tools.

Children don't seek to influence their world in pretend ways, any more than adults do. Their need to manipulate the environment is no more satisfied by pretend than an adult's need for authentic work is satisfied in online games. They may be a short-term substitute, but meaningful work is not imaginary. Meaningful work influences the real world in concrete ways, whether you're five or seventy-five.

Children want their work to be useful. They want their influence to be real. They want their contributions to be important. And so they seek (and, hopefully, we provide) the real tools to accomplish that. Whether you're a chef or a carpenter, the right tools matter. Never underestimate the importance of a quality tool in the classroom.

Offering the children the right tools for their work may be more costly in the short-term, but they're priceless in the long run. The classroom is not designed to fill the time between birth and adulthood. It's designed to equip children with the tools they need to affect their adulthood, real, quality tools with which they can do real, quality work.

It's hard to change the world with a plastic hammer. Physical tools matter. It's hard to create profound works of art if you've only been offered white paper and crayons. Creative tools matter. You cannot write great poetry if you've only ever heard sing-alongs. Intellectual tools matter. They require greater cost, both in the resources of the classroom and in our own engagement as teachers. But the return is undoubtedly worth the investment.

Grant me the faith

A servant's faith

That your vision exceeds the known horizon

Despite the limits of my imagination.

Grant me the faith

A servant's faith

That the tools you need are the ones you need

Despite the limits of my imagination.

Grant me the faith

A servant's faith

That the world you'll create will be a wondrous world

Despite the limits of my imagination.

III.   Manipulation and The Self

Think of the times when you feel out of control, when your context makes you completely dependent on factors beyond your ability to influence. There are the trivial times, stuck in traffic, or delayed by a flight pattern, or when the person in front of you at the grocery can't find the right coupons. There are the critical times, between medical tests and results, between news of the trauma and news of the survivors. The world stops in rotation. Unable to create change, unable to speed up the liminal, we pace like chained tigers. We are the emotional intersection of immoveable object and irresistible force.

Sometimes we can find the peace to use that time. We can sit in the traffic, and mentally enjoy yesterday, and mentally plan tomorrow. We can stare out the airplane's window into the darkness, and wonder from where we came, We can analyze the grocery basket ahead of us, and visualize what incredible collection of oddities must await that menu.

But usually at those moments, our lack of ability to manipulate is almost overwhelming. That friction is our need to manipulate asserting itself. Most of the time, we influence our world without even noticing. We shift in our chairs. We adjust the thermostat. We change lanes. We increase the screen size. We change our environments a thousand times a day to make them fit us a little better. It's not until we are deprived of that influence that we notice we had it. Most of the time, we take it for granted. Manipulating the world (and, indeed, the people) around us is just a part of the way the world works.

Until we can't.

Exerting our influence is an integrated, natural part of how we engage the world. Like breathing. But just as our awareness of this experience is different when we master our breath, so is our awareness richer when we master our own intent to influence it.

Observing the thousand different ways in which we try to adjust the world to our agendas, we can identify which of those we might just let go. When we attend to how often we ask the world to change to suit us, we can begin to be more intentional in choosing which changes we might make ourselves.

Our dissatisfaction, our frustration, our impatience, doesn't come from the small nuisances in the environment. It comes from our drive to control them, from our desire to make things different than they are.

When we choose to change ourselves instead of directing our focus on what's outside of us, we are no less manipulative. But our influence is far more profound.

When we choose to change ourselves, we satisfy that internal drive to change the world, to exert our control, to be in charge. But we do so in a way that leaves us, and our environment, more peaceful, more tolerant, more accepting, more grateful. When we make choices about what we need to change in ourselves and what we need to change in the world, the influence we have on the world is more intense. Our external influence can be exerted to more lasting efforts than traffic and grocery lines. We can choose to exert control over ourselves in those trivial times, and we find that we are still comforted by the outcome.

Likewise, when our context is more serious, when the challenges beyond our control are more consequential. Neither our anger nor our urgency will change the news we're waiting for. In the meantime, controlling our responses, connecting to other people who are feeling the same despair, observing our gratitude even in the midst of our crises, steels us better for whatever resolution looms. Practically, we are better prepared to respond to whatever it is that's coming if we have not spent our energies and influence on anger or impatience in the meantime.

I am unaware of my influence

What will my effect be?

I will change the world

How will I change the world?

With thermostats or extra legroom or a second cushion
behind my back?

Will my legacy be the hundred million trivial changes
I make

To make this infinite world fit me a little better?

Or the few imperceptible changes I make

To make me better fit this infinite world?

I cannot change the speed of the earth's rotation

I can control my impatience with the spin

I cannot change the other travelers around me

I can control my impatience with their spin

May I demand less

May I accept more

May I change what I can change

and know that all I can change is all I am.

IV.   Manipulation and Each Other

Our classrooms are spheres of multiple influence. We seek to create environments within which children can overlook us, but we understand that to do so requires our own careful, mindful choices. Unlike the children, we understand what parts of the environment are there by choice and which ones are the unfortunate happenstance of the culture we've inherited.

We can name the things we do on purpose and the ones that are beyond our control. And, for most of us, we prefer the things we've chosen over the ones out of our influence: the peaceful corner in which we've hung a favorite painting instead of the window too high to comfortably enjoy, the assistant teacher we recommended to be hired instead of the one we were assigned when things didn't work out in another classroom. From architecture to companionship, we are endeared to our own intentions.

Ay, there's the rub. The children, for whom these environments are so carefully prepared, do not experience them as a collection of choices and restraints. What is, is. Teachers are in classrooms. Materials are there, too.

What influences the children, then, is not whether, as teachers, we like the floor plan of the room. It's how we respond to that floor plan. The environment's health is not a factor of whether it is entirely as we would design it, but how we react to the components beyond our control. If we are constantly frustrated by the limits of our classrooms, the children will learn to be frustrated by what is beyond their control. We establish patience by modeling patience. We inspire creativity by modeling creative responses.

So, you don't like the height of that cabinet. . . chances are, there's nothing wrong with the cabinet. Chances are, it just doesn't fit with what you want for that location and it's not been installed there just to make things difficult on you. Chances are, it would be easier to change what you want than to change the height of the cabinet.

So, you don't like the way that teacher presents the Pink Tower. Chances are, there's nothing wrong with that teacher. Chances are, she understands the material differently than you do, and she's not doing what she's doing just to make things difficult on you. Chances are, it would be easier to change the disparity between how you each understand the material than to change the person with whom you teach.

When we think of the things beyond our control as somehow intending to obstruct us, we give power to the obstruction. We focus on the conflict rather than the resolution. And, too often, we come to expect that the only resolution is one which removes the obstruction rather than one which lessens its impact. When we focus on changing what's wrong rather than on what already exists that's right, we limit ourselves to a single, imagined but unrealized, outcome.

When we think of things beyond our control as, well, beyond our control, we make far more powerful use of our control. We are able to exert it on the things that we really can change, the expectations, the discrepancies, that differ between what is and what we would have be.

When we change the expectation, we lessen the discrepancy. We are more powerful, in more lasting ways, and, most importantly, in the ways we want to model for the children who, whether or not we prioritize it, are the greatest effects of our influence.

Of all the things I would change in this world

Big things

Little things

First

Let me be thing the I change in this world

Let me change my perspective

Let me change my grace

Of all the things I would leave you

Big things

Little things

First

Let me leave you better than I found you

Let me leave you patience

Let me leave you gratitude

Of all the ways the world could be

Big ways

Little ways

First

Let me see what is possible

Let me be what is possible

First in little ways

In perspective

In grace

In patience

In gratitude

Work

"An adult who does not understand that a child needs to use his hands and does not recognize this as the first manifestation of an instinct for work can be an obstacle to the child's development."

-Maria Montessori

What is your great work?

Not the tasks you do to complete each day

Not the have-to and errands and chores of survival

What is your great work

The work that defines you

That drives you?

What is your Great Work?

I. The Naming of Things: Work

Work is the thing you have to do to be able to do the thing you want to, right? Work is the toil, the labor, the struggle that you have to overcome to be able to earn time to play. Work is the most dreaded four-letter-word.

Ugh.

Work is what defines us. For most of us, that means it's how we're viewed from outside. When you meet someone, what do you ask first of them? What is your name? Where are you from? *What do you do?* We think we understand each other better by understanding the nature of each other's work.

Ah, you are an attorney. You must be very intelligent and a little bit contrary.

Ah, you are an artist. You must be creative and complicated and a little too idealistic.

Ah, you are a teacher. You must be loving and overworked and maybe sweeter than you are smart.

Because we spend so much of our lives preparing for our work, and an even greater amount of our lives doing that work, we allow ourselves to be named by it, to attribute our self-worth and the worth of others to the degree to which they influence our economy.

Think about a time when you had to do work you didn't want to do, when you had some chore that you dreaded. What did you do? Did you embrace it with passion? Did you smile throughout and wish the day would never end? Or did you finish it, completing it but never investing in it? Did you let your mind wander and imagine where you'd be when you were finally done?

Now, compare that with a time when you were doing work you *loved,* the kind that *inspired* you, when you could predict the outcome of your work and knew its importance, when you felt driven to engage, when you were called to the work. What did that work feel like? Chances are, you wouldn't even call it work. You may have gotten a paycheck, but you earned much more from it. You knew your value. You saw the outcome of your efforts. You had a concrete experience of how what you do might just change the world.

That's your great work. We all have some great work, and we are driven to it. We know how different it feels to work with purpose, with meaning (and how barren it feels when that kind of work is absent from our lives.) Though the term "work" has come to carry its own implications, to be the short-cut to the assumptions that can interfere with our understanding, our human tendency to work rises above those. Whatever the title of our *job,* we are nonetheless driven to *work.* Some of us are lucky enough to have our work and our jobs one and the same. But whether or not our great work pays our bills, its influence on our lives is unique and personal and passionate and essential. When we have not yet found our work, we hunger in its absence. When we are deeply engaged in it, we think of nothing else. When we've lived too long without it, we despair. When we are immersed in it, we inspire.

Simply, our work positions us, with ourselves and with others. We tally up how we contribute. We measure the benefit to the collective as a reflection of the individual, and in doing so, we diminish them both.

The most valuable work is not defined by salary or subordinates. Those earnings allow us only to move currency. The most valuable work is the work that draws from each of us our truest potential, that connects what we can do with how we can help. Those earnings allow us to move the universe.

II. Work and The Child

We are asked to do a lot of tasks as teachers: to take attendance, to clean the shelves, to prepare the reports, to answer the telephone calls, to make the snack, to plunge the toilets… tasks tasks tasks to keep the room going.

As Montessori teachers, we are called to do one task more carefully than others: we are called to observe the children in our care. Not in order to fill out more detailed reports or to check off more boxes on a developmental chart, but so that we can understand the child dearly, so that we can know what he knows and what he needs, so that we can use that knowledge to prepare the environment within which he can grow and thrive without us.

Observation is the key to discovering the *child's* great work, and discovering the child's great work is the key to all the rest.

We know it when we see it, when the child becomes so completely absorbed in his activity that everything else falls into place. The child who could not sit still is now focused, intent, engaged. The child whose voice was always heard above the classroom buzz is now silent, immersed, connected. The child who could never quite find something to do is now busy, attentive, absorbed.

Of all the things we know, what we don't know is the most critical: we do not know, indeed we cannot begin to envision, what the demands of the next generation will entail. No more than our parents could have imagined a world of paper thin computers and instantaneously international communication, we can only guess at what our own children will need. What we do know, with complete confidence, is that we are only seeing the very tip of a very large iceberg.

We cannot prepare our children for that unknown world by limiting them to success in this one. Instead, we prepare them by giving them the tools to persist, to focus, to discover, to become absorbed in their work, whatever their work, to find value and meaning and usefulness through engagement. We prepare them by protecting in them the one skill they most assuredly will need: the ability to learn.

And we protect that ability by offering them environments that connect their learning to their work, that ask of them endurance and reflection and experimentation. Despite the speed of the world around us, learning doesn't have a single data rate. There is no stopwatch on knowledge.

When the children are "at work," in our classrooms, they are learning to learn. When they find their great work, they are experiencing learning in its most powerful incarnation, when what they do becomes essential to who they are, when the difference between what their work does for others and what it does for themselves is indistinguishable.

It's a thrilling and addicting experience, one which we seek to replicate throughout our lives, when the difference between what our work does for others and what it does for ourselves are one and the same.

The child's great work may not be what we would choose for him, and we must understand, as teachers, parents, caregivers, that our goal is not to define the work for the child, but to help him to discover it for himself. We care for our children when we give them the tools to design their own lives, not when we force them into the boxes we've constructed long before they were born. We serve our children when we create environments within which the unimaginable future can take form, when the possibilities beyond our ability to conceive become real.

You have more within you than I will ever be

Hiding

Unseeable

Immeasurable

Potential

May I handle your future gently

May I distinguish between protection and limitation

May I help you to discover the work that drives you

The work that connects you

That engages and absorbs you

That Great Work

Your Great Work

May I handle you gently

III.   Work and The Self

When we're children, there's little difference between work and play. Everything we do, from the crayons with which we make our masterpieces to the songs we sing to remember which shoe goes on which foot, is both. We are working toward becoming whatever it is we are going to become, and we are developing that, often, through play.

There is some shift, inevitably, when we "grow up." Work becomes work and play becomes play. We wear different clothes, special uniforms, to demonstrate our professionalism. We use different names for ourselves to distinguish our titles and positions. We speak differently, write differently, engage differently. We forget, as we spend more and more time in this extended game of dress-up, that it's pretend. We have separated what we do from who we are, and in the doing, have distanced ourselves from our authentic lives. We are left, instead, with complicated games of make-believe.

And what do we do when we're "off work?" We breathe out. We slouch. We put up our feet and put on the tube and disengage even further. Our work has not always left us inspired. It hasn't always given us a sense of rightness or realness or authenticity. We are no more full or fulfilled. We are, too often, still hungry.

When our work engages us, we are engaged in more than the task at hand. Our entire selves are absorbed in the task. We have purpose and usefulness and authenticity.

And it doesn't matter what the work is, as long as it is our work.

For some of us, authentic work is with the hand, gardening, building, painting. It's work that engages our bodies and our minds together in creating something new. For some of us, authentic work is in the mind, sorting out a mathematical equation or constructing the perfect combination of words.

Whatever is your authentic work ,it is that work that makes the world make more sense. It creates what is good, or removes what is wrong. Authentic work drives us because it speaks to our higher selves. At some level, we understand that it is about more than the have-tos of daily life. It is not about getting bills paid or checking off boxes in our to-do lists. It helps us to understand our human existence on some deeper, if often unspoken level.

Which is not to say that it takes the place of the work we have to do. Indeed, it is often because we do the work we don't want to do that we are able to do the work that we fulfills us. Most of us need to find some balance between the practical and the profound. But we do need to find that balance.

All too often, we lean toward logistics and turn away from the horizon of our hearts. We spend our time distracting ourselves from that hunger, as though if we keep ourselves just busy enough the gnawing feeling will go away or we'll just get used to it. And we do get used to it. Like any chronic pain, we learn to accept it as the new normal. Like any chronic pain, we allow ourselves to numb. Like any chronic pain, if we don't address it, it won't go away. We must find the courage to address it, to make the time, to demand it of our lives, for work that satisfies us.

When we find the means to work our authentic work, we find the path back to the potential we had before we grew up, before we traded in our childhood games for their less playful adult versions. We rediscover our real purpose, our authentic lives, far better than any game of make-believe.

Grant me

Courageous Action

Purposeful Work

Authentic Life

Grant me balance from the tempting numbness

Return me to my childhood's enthusiasm

To my confidence that I am a creator

That I can make the world make sense

That I can make the world a better place

Grant me the daring to seek my authentic work

And the insight to embrace it when I do

IV.   Work and Each Other

We spend most of our day in the company of our coworkers, those powerful people whose influence can make our work a playground or a battlefield. And each of us knows which of the people in our workplace to seek out and which ones to avoid. A healthy coworker can make the most tedious requirements fly by. A tedious coworker can make us dread even the most fulfilling work. We know them apart. We can name them, and we know how deeply they affect our work.

Our work, whether or not we like it, is intimate to us. And because we are so intimately tied to our workplaces, we are equally tied, whether or not we like it, to the people with whom we work. We carry the struggles we endure with them into our private lives. We find our value or question it by their contributions.

How often, though, do we ask ourselves which kind of coworker we are? As we grumble and gossip about the colleagues we don't like, as we complain about differences in personality or procedure, do we ask ourselves whether we may be the problem?

Or are we mostly comfortable presuming that, but for the presence of that one annoyance in our workplace, things would be much better off? When our workplace, that intimate environment to which we give so much and from which we draw in equal amounts, is more work than joy, how often do we ask if the responsibility is ours?

Our work, whether or not we like it, is intimate to us. If for no other cause than the abundance of our time that's dedicated to it, it reflects us. It evokes our strengths and our weaknesses. When there is strife there, we feel it dearly. When there is joy, we are joyful. But that intimacy also gives us the opportunity to strengthen more than our professional trajectory by our contributions there.

Too often, we see the challenging behavior of children as the result of some imposed obstacle to their ability to demonstrate their natural condition: peaceful, collaborative, joyful. At what point do we stop presuming that of each other? At what point do we stop looking for the imposed obstacle and start blaming the person?

How different our conflicts would be if, instead of presuming that other person is the cause of our stress, we looked for the changes we could make in ourselves that would allow them to return to their natural condition: peaceful, collaborative, joyful.

Our work, whether or not we like it, is intimate to us. When we see our work environments as places in which we are called to bring out the best in each other, we will bring out the best in each other. When we see our work as being more than the tasks we have to do, but the collective work of human engagement, we can accomplish more than the daily checklists of our job descriptions. When we recognize that we are as essential a component of whether our workplace is peaceful, or not, or collaborative, or not, or joyful, or not, we set ourselves on a path toward our own natural condition.

There was some point at which we began seeing each other as the problem. That way of seeing then itself becomes the problem. Remove it, and we can get back to the way we are meant to be.

My work is my mirror

May I offer to it what I want reflected to me

Seeking joy, may I offer joy.

Seeking compassion, may I offer compassion.

Seeking strength, may I offer strength.

Seeking forgiveness, may I offer forgiveness.

May I be a person I want to work with

And, in doing, discover them in abundance around me

Repetition

"It is exactly in the repetition of the exercises that the education of the senses exists; not that the child shall know colors, forms or qualities, but that he refine his senses through an exercise of attention, comparison and judgment."

- Maria Montessori

What are your best habits?

What are the ones you wish you could change?

Which of your quirks make you distinctly you?

Which would you rather were another's?

I. The Naming of Things: Repetition

We are best defined not by the ways we wish we were, but by the habits that we barely recognize. The things we do by rote, the routines and rituals that are so deeply engrained that, although we never think of them, we would immediately notice if they were broken.

We may initially establish routines to satisfy the mundane. Where exactly are my keys? Have I taken my medicine today? Where did I leave my phone? By doing things the same way, over and over and over, we make sure nothing falls through the cracks. We create predictability. We get out of the house on time. We stop misplacing things. But over time, these routines come to describe us. We are as reliable as the way we live our lives. Other people come to know us by the habits we keep. Our rituals overlap with theirs. We become to rely on them, as comforts and assurances.

Our tendency toward repetition reflects the neediest parts of our spirits: those doubtful little wonderings, "Will the world work today as it worked yesterday? And tomorrow? And in this moment? And this one?" We are testing our environment, sometimes consciously but more often not, to assure ourselves that things are reliable. We are safe. We are secure. We are sound.

Don't confuse useful repetition with idiosyncrasies, or superstitions, or old wives' tales. Some won't ever drink from a straw, or step on the cracks, or dance with a stranger. These may be habitual acts, but they are not the repetitions that lead us toward our betterment.

And in our efforts to soothe ourselves, we create a space of comfort for each other. I may not know the name of the man behind me at the coffee shop, but I know I see him there most Tuesdays. I know my neighbor walks her two dogs up the opposite side of our street and back home on the same side as mine. There is a crossing guard who automatically holds traffic for me when I'm out for a run. I say good morning to him almost every day, and I know when he's not there that school must be out. This places me, in my day, in my community, in my life, in a reliable, sound, space, that includes other people who know me as reliably as I know them. None of them are really dear to me. But each is essential.

There are endless ways in which we are inconsequential. Few of us are likely to change the world in the ways that get noticed, in discoveries that alter the field of physics or great works that redefine modern art. Lost in the relatively inappreciable impact we make, we hunger for reminders that we affect something, no matter how trivial that something may be. We repeat our influence for the same purpose as ground-breaking scientific experiments are repeated: to be certain of them.

Our tendency toward repetition satisfies our need for certainty in a world that leaves us, more often than not, with reminders of our insignificance. The crossing guard, the dog walker, the man with his coffee, they remind us that our lives are a part of something bigger than ourselves, that we are connected, even if in only very small ways, as part of a universal routine. We develop routines to satisfy the mundane. We maintain them to satisfy the sublime.

II. Repetition and The Child

From almost as soon as an infant is able to take intentional action, she begins to repeat it. The tendency toward repetition in infants is easy to observe. Throw the toy. Wait for a parent to retrieve the toy. Throw the toy. Wait for a parent to retrieve the toy. Repeat. Repeat. Repeat.

When those actions result in some effect, they are repeated. Throw the toy. The parent engages. Aha! The toy results in the parent's engagement! Success! The child throws the toy again. When those actions have no effect, they are often quickly cast aside. The child cries. No one responds. Over time, the child stops crying.

The infant, without any means to classify the world, tests it. Is this a reliable place? Is this a place in which my needs will be met? Am I safe here? And the world provides those answers. And sometimes they're the ones we want the infant to hear. And sometimes not. When I cry, will someone comfort me? When I am scared, will someone soothe me? Am I part of something bigger than I am, or am I on my own?

As the infant grows, that same need to test the environment grows, as well. The infant's repetition provides immediate comfort and assurance. The child's repetition teaches him about his influence.

To what degree can I change the world? The Montessori classroom offers an ideal answer: to whatever degree you choose. The environment, designed not only to give children an opportunity to develop specific skills for their own independence, also grants them whatever time they need, uninterrupted, to repeat those efforts until the child's inner drive is satisfied. We don't reprimand the child who is working for "too long" with rice pouring. We don't tell children they are not allowed to use the long rods any more because they've already done them. We allow children to duplicate their work, understanding that the child who repeats an activity does so because he is driven to that repetition.

Children repeat activities to provide a safe place from which to explore, to rest on a new plateau from which to advance, to establish a comfort and confidence after which they are able to take on greater challenges. That repetition may be a part of the child's daily routine. Enter the room. Choose the spooning work. Complete it before you begin something new.

Children also repeat activities when they are learning new concepts, when they are internalizing new ideas for the first time and testing them to understand their nature more deeply. Build the tower. Deconstruct it. Build it again. That repetition may be immediate, again and again all morning long.

Finally, children repeat activities when they are in retreat, when they need to be reminded of their safe harbor. Put aside the trinomial charts and find instead the knobbed cylinders. That repetition may be a cycle of the year, when the child who has advanced to complicated materials and relationships reverts to the oasis of familiar, simple tasks. Every so often, we all have to stop, to take a breath, to retreat, before we move forward.

In each cycle, the child's tendency to repeat provides an assurance to her. And when that repetition is supported, the child's questions are answered clearly. The world is a safe place in which your influence is felt. The people around you are reliable and value your contribution. You are safe. You are warm. You are loved.

With every action

You question

With every reaction

I respond

May I offer comfort

When you ask for a reliable world

May I be worthy of your trust

When you ask not to be alone

May I be a worthy companion

With every action

You question

With every reaction

May I respond

III.   Repetition and The Self

We don't really grow out of the need for repetition. We just develop less noticeable ways to satisfy it. While the infant may frustrate his mother with airborne spoonfuls of mashed peas, we hide our need for repetition in useful, practical habits and call them efficiency. It doesn't save the peas, but it helps create the child.

We hang our coats in the same places and leave our planners on the same spot on our desks. We have a special place for our car keys or our phones. (Or we don't, and we have, instead, a frustrating ritual of looking for them every day.) Even the constant adventurers, those road warriors who trade the luxury of a key hook for a perpetual journey, look closely: they have their own rituals, too. Theirs are just portable.

In childhood, our tendency toward repetition helps us to find our place in the world. As adults, our more subtle rituals help us to maintain it. Where we sit in the morning to drink that first cup of coffee, or follow the usual path of our favorite walk through the neighborhood, these are the little rituals of our lives and, like all ritual, they serve to keep us connected in a concrete, tangible way to the universe around us. They situate us in time and space and relationship to each other.

Those rituals are not always a choice, actively made between equal alternatives. When we lack them, we lack our connection to the universal cycle. We are out of sorts, out of time, off the beat. We know there is something wrong, but we don't know exactly what it is that's so unsettling. We attribute our dis-ease to stress, or finances, or a lack of time.

Montessori is a practice rich in ritual. Each presentation we offer, so carefully practiced to assure that each finger is in the right location, each gesture and movement analyzed to be sure it is the most efficient to accomplish any given task. This is ritual.

As children, repetition assures of the world. As adults, ritual assures us of our contribution to it. Some of those rituals are the ones that make our contribution stronger, that fortify our ability to endure and persist and engage in ways that make our world stronger. Some of our rituals are ones that tear us down, that erode us.

Our classroom rituals are intentional. How we welcome with our handshakes the children into the classroom, and the songs we sing together, and the way we say goodbye. This is ritual. The names we use for each other and the special terms we use to describe ourselves. This is ritual. It forms the skeleton of Montessori upon which all the messy, spontaneous, unplanned and chaotically human interactions hang.

If we are to give some structure to the messiness that is our own lives, we must start with the rituals that tie it together. In our classrooms, these are conscious, practiced choices. In our lives, they should be, too. In our classrooms, these are daily engagements. In our lives, they must be, too. We are often so focused on the preparation of our environments that we forget that we must also prepare ourselves. *What we repeat, we become.* And what we become, we bring with us to the children. If we are to provide for them the reliable comfort of a predictable world, we have to be sure of it ourselves.

I am called to mind, to mirror, to model

I am called to mind the child

To offer her my attention

My attentiveness

My comfort and consolation

I am called to mirror the world

To reflect a predictable, reliable universe

To evidence the clockworks through my steady beat

I am called to model the rhythm

To contribute regardless of the magnitude of my
contribution

To be part of the whole I will always be too small to see

May I mind, mirror, model

With purpose

With care

With assurance

For myself and for the child

IV.   Repetition and Each Other

We may appreciate the comfort our routines give us in our own lives, but we probably don't think as deeply about the impact they may have on other people. More likely, we are aware of the ways in which *their* rituals affect us, but not quite as attentive to the ways in which ours support or, perhaps just as likely, obstruct theirs.

Think about something that *always* annoys you. Is it the way your coteacher leaves her water bottle on the shelf? Or how your neighbor parks just a little too close to your driveway? Or where your children drop their backpacks at the end of the day? These little nuisances, which seem to us to be small things that a more thoughtful person could change, are habits that provide routine and its resulting comfort to the people around us, even as they annoy us. And like anything which has become habit, they're difficult to undo.

Think of something you do that always annoys the people around you. Maybe a little harder to name? We're rarely as conscious of the unease we cause than the irritation we feel. We trust that we aren't living our lives with any intent of bothering the people around us. We'd do well to presume the same of others.

Think of something that always helps you to be your best. Maybe it's time with a particular friend. Maybe it's time alone to reflect. Maybe it's regular exercise or meditation. What is a small way you might begin to make more of that in your life? Habits begin as small choices. Think of something you do that *always* brings the best out in the people around you. Maybe it's listening more carefully. Maybe it's reminding others of the good you see in them. Maybe it's offering encouragement instead of critique. What is a small way you might begin to make more of that in other's lives? Small choices can evoke extraordinary changes.

All too often, we presume that the people who obstruct us do so by choice. If we want our environment to be one of peace, we are bound to act peacefully. All too often, we presume that the people who hurt us do so by choice. If we want our environment to be one of forgiveness, we are honor bound to forgive. All too often, we want grand gestures of reconciliation and overlook the small efforts that yield more lasting influence. If we want our resplendent rituals to offer us meaning and purpose, we must choose our daily habits with no less noble intent.

What is one thing you could change today, one small thing, one practically imperceptible adjustment that might make things just a little tiny bit better? Start there. Do that little thing, that negligible effort, every day until even you no longer notice it. Hold the door open. Say, "Good Morning" to someone you usually don't. Empty the dishwasher.

Then, find something a little bigger. Think of something a little less subtle. Do that. Do that every day until it, too, becomes what you are.

When we change our habits, we change those defining patterns that describe us to others and illustrate the way we view the world. When we change our habits, we change who we are. We change who we are to each other. We change what we are to the universe. And that little thing, that practically imperceptible influence becomes a little tiny bit better. It's a start.

Today

In this moment

In this boundless universe

In this endless expanse of time and space

In this indescribably vast out there out there

I am small

I am inconsequential

Unnoticeable and unseen

Today

In this moment

In this boundless universe

In this endless expanse of time and space

In this indescribably vast out there out there

I am essential

I am intrinsic

Paramount and primary

May I choose small actions

With the faith of great influence

Precision

"A child who is free to act not only seeks to gather sensible impressions from his environment but he also shows a love for exactitude in the carrying out of his actions."

- Maria Montessori

What are the essential parts of your teaching?

What are those pieces of your practice that, without which, your teaching would no longer be your teaching?

What are the extraneous tasks you wish you could do without?

I. The Naming of Things: Precision

Exactness. Precision. What do these words mean? We see them used in advertisements all the time. Fine objects are crafted with precision and to our exact specifications. We have a sense of the handiwork that's involved in exactness. We can imagine a machine tuned with precision. But the words themselves demand clarity. What a laugh we'd have if we were to talk about precision and exactness in vague, ambiguous ways.

Exactness. From the Latin *exactus*, to drive out. Precision. From the Latin *praecīsiō,* a cutting off.

When we work toward exactness, we drive out what is not necessary. We cut off what is extraneous. We edit. We refine. We sharpen.

And we are left with what is essential. What is core. What is atomic.

What happens when you boil down a broth? You evaporate the water. You are left with what is essential. What is core. In the boiling down, you are rewarded with a new intensity of flavor, a sublime integration of taste. The heart of the matter.

What happens when we boil down our practice? When we evaporate what is unnecessary? We are left with what is essential. What is core. In the boiling down, we are rewarded with a new intensity of intent, a sublime integration of engagement.

The tendency toward exactness calls us to refine to the essential, to the atomic, to that powerful core of our teaching which best defines us. What are the distinct, unique, and personal ways in which I stand alone? What are the exact means of my influence? When we identify with precision which parts of our teaching are essential and which parts are extraneous, we drive out what interferes and we are left with our atomic core, that dynamic essence that distinguishes us from the messy, distracted chaos of our society. Here I am. This is me.

Throughout our classrooms, we offer children what is real, what is accurate, what is precise. When we are criticized for the mechanical sterility of our materials, we quietly reply that it is not through chaos that we create. Think of the great works of art, the ones that still stand generation after generation. They rivet our attention because, despite the limits of culture or context or time, we understand them. They speak to the core of our human experience. They are profound because they articulate what is essential. In our teaching, when we begin with what is essential, we offer the child what is common to the human experience. It is in that common experience where lasting creativity takes root.

Whether we're making great art or good soup, that's where we need to begin. When we start with the essential, we allow for the profound.

II. Precision and The Child

Children in our classrooms expect us to provide precise, carefully planned environments. When routines are disrupted, they point it out. When materials are returned to the wrong place on the shelf, they notice. When the reliability we have assured them is missing, they let us know. And further, in their own work, they seek an internal consistency, an exactness of placement and alignment. They shift the tiniest cube so it sits perfectly centered on the top of the tower. They carefully place the prisms of the trinomial cube and maintain the order of the cylinders.

That is, when they have been allowed to do so.

For the very young child, exactness begets exactness. When children are offered an environment within which their tendency toward exactness can be satisfied, they mirror that precision in their own actions. But remember: exactness is the hidden tendency, the one that, when satisfied, we barely notice anymore. For the child who is never offered such precision, there is an evident, chronic unease. Lacking a model for precision, he is cacophonous and disorderly.

The child needs our lens to make sense of the loud, colorful, busy world spinning around her. She relies on us to help her focus, to find quiet in the midst of all that chaos. If we don't provide that refinement for her, we don't remove the need. We just give her fewer tools with which to satisfy the hunger.

That's why Montessori classrooms serve such a wide range of children so well. . . we don't presume that a child has already internalized that necessary exactness. Instead, we offer it explicitly throughout the classroom and to every child. Each lesson, carefully presented, precisely offered. Each word, limited and chosen for its exact and concise meaning. Each material, one of a kind, designed to do what it does and only what it does. It is through this carefully designed external environment that the child internalizes and satisfies the need for exactness. It's from that place of internal exactness that the child's most creative energies emerge.

Remember: exactness and chaos are a matched set. To the child in chaos, we offer precision. To the child who has internalized that precision, we offer endless opportunities to expand to the absolute limits of his own innovation. Scientist and Artist, the child needs our model of exactness to understand the world and to build upon it. We cannot create in his place. That is only ever his work. But we can provide for him the environment within which to create, the reliable, exact, refined, precise integration of concepts and ideas from which his own artistry will emerge.

You come to me seeking balance.

May I greet you with balance.

You come to me seeking precision

May I greet you with precision

You come to me seeking exactness

May I greet you with exactness

When you are flooded by chaos

May I remember how very chaotic this world must feel

When you're so small and stuck in the middle of it

When you are flooded

May I offer you a still, solid rock

Reliable and sound

On which to perch

From which to watch the waters flow

May I calm your storm

May I offer balance

Precision

Exactness

III.   Precision and The Self

If you've ever, in a fit of stress or procrastination, decided to sort out all your dresser drawers or reorganize your closet, you've experienced the tendency toward exactness. Overwhelmed by a new task or frustrated by not knowing where to begin on a new project, we throw ourselves instead into tidying our environment. Once the physical, external space is precisely prepared, we may be better suited to express our own creativity within it.

Most of the time, our need for exactness is met through the reliable structures of our lives. We adjust the painting to hang straight on the wall. We flatten the sheets before making the bed. In small ways, through almost invisible, easily overlooked gestures, we protect the precision of the environments within which we live. We seek efficiency in our routines. We seek exactness.

And when we have met our need for exactness, we barely notice it. Like the hidden gears of a well-crafted watch, that precision allows us to move through our lives without it ever drawing our attention. Indeed, it is not until it's absent that we may even be able to name the ways in which we relied upon it. And why we miss it so.

What then? What do we do when our lives are thrown into chaos, when the internal exactness we have developed over years is no longer available to us? Just as we would for the children, we need to retreat, to observe what is missing and prepare an environment within which it can be found. We have come in from the cold. A crisis at school keeps us from our regular three-hour work cycle. We can meet that chaos with chaos, or we can balance it with exactness.

Unfortunately, it's not in just the big crises that we need to find the space for precision and exactness. When the chaos in our lives is at an extreme, so should be our intentional efforts at exactness. But when the chaos is manageable, that doesn't mean the exactness is gone. We still search for it. We just satisfy the need in more subtle ways.

Consider the Practical Life shelves: without regular maintenance, the rice gets dusty, the water gets stagnant, the beans go missing. We prevent that by attending to the materials daily. In the same way, we need to attend to our own need for precision daily. Luckily, we can do so while we're preparing our environments. . . a necessary requirement of the job happens also to be quite healthy for us! Regularly taking the time to clean our shelves, to count the beads in our math materials or replenish the water in our pouring vessels: these are small gestures that increase the precision of the classroom and, in turn, the exactness in our own lives. When we contribute to an orderly environment around us, even in small ways, we satisfy our own tendency toward exactness at the same time.

Find the small things toward which you can increase your precision. Perhaps it's in preparing materials to make sure new materials on the shelf are designed with specificity and exactness. Perhaps it's in counting materials at the end of each day to make sure every bead is accounted for. Perhaps it's in cutting paper to fit the metal inset bases precisely, no matter which way the square is oriented. When we take the time to complete small tasks with great attentiveness, we establish environments that allow both children and teachers to thrive.

I am sloppy

disorganized

unkempt

I fly by the seat of my pants

And hold on by the skin of my teeth

Trying to keep pace with the momentum of my world

May I remember that precision of the well-crafted
timepiece

The carefully measured gears

Working in perfect coordination

Must be carefully set

Before the clock is wound

Stop. Calibrate. Wind.

IV.   Precision and Each Other

Our tendency toward exactness may be the most difficult to observe. By its nature, when our drive to exactness is fulfilled, it becomes so integrated to our lives that it seems to disappear. But have no doubt: it's there. There is an architecture to our lives, a well-ordered precision within which the glorious chaos of our everyday can unfold.

Here is the central thesis: chaos and exactness often appear as a matched set. The more you have of one, the more you seek of the other. In science, we seek a balance between the creative idea and the accuracy of the experiment to test it. In art, we contain the innovation within specific parameters, the frame, the base, the canvas. Artist or scientist or both, we are driven toward exactness throughout our lives.

Exactness is a necessary component of human society. It's what allows for our technology, our buildings, our innovations great and small. It allows us to build towers that rise above the clouds and to perform surgery with only the tiniest of incisions. It allows doors to close without squeaking and whispers to be heard around the world. The technological advancements that distinguish us from other mammals are not the result of haphazard trial and error: they reflect our deep and intentional precision, our efforts to become more exact, more reliable and more refined.

In science, we seek simpler, more precise ways to understand the universe. In art, we seek simpler, more precise ways to articulate that understanding. Knowledge evolves toward precision, in lifetimes and over human development. Even our efforts at precision evolve toward greater precision. Computers that used to take up entire floors of buildings can now fit in the space of a fingernail. Over time, over generations, we move toward exactness.

Some of us are the hapless beneficiaries of the precision around us, floating unaware of the exactness upon which we rely so heavily.

Beware: one flat tire and the illusion is over. None of us is truly separate from the human need for precision. Our efforts at exactness, indeed, are a lifelong preparation of our environment, a setting-up so that we can take action. We seek exactness in order not to need it. If the mechanics of an innovation work seamlessly, we are able to enjoy those innovations without ever thinking of what went in to their development. And when they are absent, when we have not prepared our own environments with precision or engaged in our own tasks with attention and care, we find ourselves easily flustered. Things don't work the way they should. There's a noise. There's a rattle. There's a psychic unease, a misalignment that keeps us from feeling steady.

I have lost my scarf. It is not on the hook where I always leave it. I search for it every day. Not so much because I especially loved the scarf, but because it was not on that hook.

When we are attentive, though, to our need for exactness, we are better suited to prepare for it. Our need for precision is a tendency better maintained than remediated. Look around. Is there order and exactness in the environment? Do things function properly? Do the pieces all fit together seamlessly? And if they don't, what changes can be made to increase their precision? How can we speak with more clarity? How can we boil down our practice to what is core? From where do we find our atomic essence, the place from which our greatest influence emerges?

The presence of that precision may never be noticed, but its absence can never, ever be ignored.

How do I prepare the environment for my own experience?

I'm on my own. No scientist observing my tendencies

No servant preparing the space.

No saint to model.

For the children, I prepare an environment free of external obstacles.

I make exacting choices of materials and presentation.

I choose my words and actions with precision.

For my teaching, may I prepare the same.

An environment free of external obstacles.

May I make exacting choices in what I draw out and what I cut off.

May I choose my words and actions with other adults with the same precision as I offer the child.

For my life, may I prepare the same.

An environment free of external obstacles.

May I make exacting choices in what I draw out and what I cut off.

May I choose my words and my actions with myself with the same precision as I offer the child.

Abstraction

"Children show a great attachment to the abstract subjects when they arrive at them through manual activity. They proceed to fields of knowledge hitherto held inaccessible to them, as grammar and mathematics."

- Maria Montessori

What is your fairy tale?

Who are your heroes?

Who rides the gallant steed?

What is the world of your imagination like?

How far far away is your real life from the life you imagine?

I. The Naming of Things: Abstraction

Of all the Tendencies, it is our Tendency toward Abstraction that is most quintessentially human, the one that distinguishes us most clearly from our animal counterparts. Our drive toward abstraction is our drive toward creativity, toward poetry, toward the unknown and unknowable. It allows us to envision the future and sympathize with the distant path, to make choices whose impact we will never personally feel, to live beyond ourselves and beyond our immediate experiences. Our tendency toward abstraction allows us to create endless worlds inside our minds, long before we ever go about making them real.

Abstraction, simply, is our ability to envision in our mind's eye that which is not in our tangible world. Our memories are abstractions. So, too, are our emotions. Our hopes and dreams. And, more practically, our ability to read with comprehension, or to complete mathematical operations "in our heads," to think out the best route to a restaurant or to remember where we left our keys- these are all examples of our abstract mind at work.

In our daily lives, abstraction allows us to function within a larger context than the physical environment around us. We can remember tasks we were to accomplish and plan for how to get them done. We can make choices about the order of activities, consider options, and make choices. We can exist beyond our immediate needs and outside of our immediate concrete environments.

Abstraction gives us memory, language, connection. It allows us to share with each other across generations or cultures, to capture complex emotions in a perfect metaphor or a cacophonous musical phrase. It allows us to capture what is sublime and what is universal and what is, essentially, human. It is the tendency of imagination.

And, as a reflection of our own evolution as complex beings, abstraction relies on a foundation of what is real, what is concrete, what is temporal. Without understanding what is mundane, we can never identify the sublime. Without understanding how the world works now, we can't imagine how to move toward a new future.

Think of the great works of art, the ones that remain poignant and evocative over hundreds of years and across societies. Art is profound when it speaks to the common human experience. This painting conveys the struggles of motherhood. This sculpture expresses lost love. This music evokes mourning.

But to articulate that experience, one must understand it. To articulate an alternative, one must know to what it is opposed. The tendency toward abstraction begins with our immediate knowledge of the concrete. By first experiencing being a mother or a child, we are able to express that beautiful tension abstractly. By first knowing love, we are able to express more aptly its loss.

II. Abstraction and The Child

Children demonstrate the tendency toward abstraction as soon as they begin to develop special relationships with other people. Once their motivations move beyond food, or sleep, or comfort, they begin to use their abstract minds. They know *this* face means *father. That* face means *mother.* These are faces to be trusted. These are faces to reach for. These are relationships on which I can rely.

For the very young child, that is perhaps the most important abstraction, the singular lesson to be learned: beyond my physical needs, which are the relationships on which I can rely? The child, coming to us with no understanding of how the world works or his own place within it, spends the first year integrating his concrete experiences into a strongly held abstraction that reflects his new understanding and the role he believes himself to play. The child draws abstract conclusions from her concrete experiences, and, in turn, learns whether this world is one in which she is safe and one on which she can rely. That abstraction will shadow or propel her long beyond her infancy.

Whether in relationships or number systems, the child expands her concrete experiences into a generalized, abstract knowledge that will, in turn, inform how she experiences the rest of her life. Abstraction is a subtle tendency, though. It is the sum conclusion of a thousand small concrete experiences. We do not come to understand the *idea* of a tree by seeing a *single* tree. We come to understand it by seeing *thousands* of trees, in all their different forms, some small, some large, some green, some red, some with fruit, some with needles. After a thousand small experiences, we finally understand the idea of a tree.

It is no small mandate, then, for the adults who serve the child to make certain that those thousand small concrete experiences teach the lessons we intend for her to learn. If we want the child to learn to trust in us and the world, we must, in a thousand small ways, demonstrate that we can be trusted. If we want the child to trust her own capacity to contribute, we must, in a thousand small ways, offer her the opportunity to experience her efficacy in action. If we want the child to learn to resolve conflicts peacefully, we must, in a thousand small ways, model peaceful resolution. No one example is enough. Abstraction is the aggregate of the countless concrete experiences of a concept, through which the child constructs her knowledge of the world.

We must envision the prepared environment as wall-less, moving far beyond those specific didactic materials on our shelves. The prepared environment incorporates not only the precise, beautiful manipulative, but the ways in which we engage with children, the language we use, the tone of our voices, the angle of our bodies. If we want the child to learn that the world is a place in which other human beings will welcome her warmly, engage her authentically, love her unceasingly, we must offer that to her in a thousand small ways. We must prepare ourselves, as an essential part of the environment, in a thousand small ways. We must exist as though the child is always watching, because the child *is* always watching. The most important lessons we teach are sometimes the ones we didn't know we were teaching.

My every action

My every word

Becomes a part of how you understand the world

May I be peaceful

That you learn peace.

May I be trustworthy,

That you learn to trust.

May I be loving,

That you learn how deeply you are loved.

My every action

My every word

Becomes a part of who you are

Let my fingerprints be gentle

Let my guidance be true

Let me be the person I say I am

That you become the person you may become

III.   Abstraction and The Self

As adults, those critical lessons we learned as children become our way of being in the world. Those thousand small ways in which we found ourselves supported or abandoned, encouraged or disdained, influence the choices we make, the people we value, the ones we avoid. Even when we acknowledge that we may view the world in ways we want to change, that acknowledgment is nonetheless a part of the engagement.

We are cautious, or in any event we should be, with the types of experiences we protect for children. As Montessorians, we avoid obstructing their development, understanding that the trajectory of the child's natural path is far more powerful than we could design for him. As adults, responsible now for our own trajectory, we we should be equally cautious of the conclusions we inadvertently preserve and the ones which might be better discarded. For children, we demonstrate this caution by preparing a carefully designed environment, within which each material is thoughtfully chosen to match the developing needs of the specific children the environment serves.

For example, we are certain that the manipulatives are in perfectly working order, that the shelves are tidy, that the tools she needs to accomplish her work are readily available, that the placement of choices is orderly and predictable. We understand that the child's concrete experiences are helping to form her abstract mind, and so we construct concrete experiences which support the abstractions we intend. How often do we offer the same care to our concrete experiences as adults? How careful are we with our own prepared environment? Look around your space right now. Is it an environment that leads you to order, to security, to peace? Are the tools you need to accomplish your goals available to you? What lessons does it teach about your value, your ability to contribute, your importance? What tasks are prioritized? Which ones are missing?

While our adult minds may be more refined in their ability to abstract, our spirits are no less deeply affected by the concrete environments we experience. This is the hidden danger of the tendency toward abstraction: our complicated imaginations can trick us into thinking the concrete environment doesn't matter anymore. But our tendency toward abstraction is never finished… we are always dancing between the lofty worlds of our minds and the mundane demands of the everyday. We may not want, or indeed be able to, restrain the sublime horizons of our abstract minds, but we can make the disparity less extreme by preparing concrete environments that support them. Our ability to integrate those binary lenses lies in closing the distance between the lives we imagine and the ones we live.

When we prepare our environment as adults, we offer ourselves the same courtesy we intend when we prepare the environment for the children. We believe, for the child, that the prepared environment helps to provide the concrete experiences that establish certain habits of mind, preserve certain paradigms of efficacy, cooperation and peace, and construct firm foundations from which future development can unfold. For ourselves, as adults, a carefully prepared environment allows for certain habits of mind, reinforces our paradigms of efficacy, cooperation and peace, and fortifies the foundation on which our creativities rely. To translate our theoretical imaginings, of how the world might work or how we may contribute to it, back into concrete action, we need a seamless balance between our abstract minds and our material environment. In children, we prepare the environment to support the abstraction. As adults, we strengthen the abstraction by aligning the environment.

I seek peace

Surrounded by noise

I seek control

Surrounded by chaos

I hold things

Papers

Objects

Lists

As though these things will move me toward the life I
want to lead

But things can't move me

Papers can't move me

Objects and lists can't move me

Seeking control

May I create it in myself first

Seeking it first in myself

May I create it in my environment

Seeking peace

May I create it in myself first

Seeking it first in myself

May I create it in my environment

May I prepare for the world I want to create

By preparing the environment within which it can flourish

IV.   Abstraction and Each Other

How is it that teachers, trained in the same method and arguably valuing the same qualities of education and children's development, can disagree so often and so passionately? How can we read the same words and understand them so differently? How can we all observe the same child and debate so vehemently his nature?

The method may be the same. Our understanding of it is not. The qualities of education and children's development may be objectively named, but they are nonetheless internalized for each of us in highly subjective, individualized ways. None of us sees the world through exactly the same eyes. Even when we share experiences, we share them through the distinct and unique and incomparable context of our own emotions, our parenting, our demographics, and all the other immeasurable and even unnamable ways in which our lives are distinctly our own. Abstraction, that singular language unique to each individual mind, prevents us from ever truly understanding another person's experience, even as it compels us to sympathize nonetheless.

And because our view of the world, our understanding of why what happens happens and who is to take the credit or the blame, is so essential and authentic to us, we can sometimes forget that it is no more *real* than any other person's view. It is real to us, because it is the abstract result of the concrete lives we have led, but unless we're living in a community of psychics, it is often foreign and hidden from each other. We easily discard each other's conclusions for being misguided or miseducated or just not quite as informed as ours are. We easily discard the truth they articulate because it counters our own. We discard the person.

When our abstract understandings of the world collide, we may be best to return to the concrete. What is objective? What can be experienced with our hands, in our environment, with evidence beyond our own experience? Absent the judgments and conclusions of our abstract minds, what is *concrete?* Without the discretion and judgment of our own experience, what is *material?* When we are engaged in theoretical arguments, the best resolutions are the ones that step back from the theories to which we've already committed and instead observe with care the concrete experiences that informed them.

Seeking peace in this way demands humility, from the Latin *humilis* or "lowly." We spend our lives reaching for something higher, elevating our thinking, striving for the world of our imagination. What a challenge, then, that in order to move higher, sometimes we have to make ourselves lowly. Humility is not the same as shame, though. Stepping away from the certainty of our conclusions to find the commonality of our experiences does not mean those conclusions we held were invalid or even suspect. But it allows us the opportunity to test them, both for our own momentum and for our communion with others. It grounds us. To walk together in the same direction, we need to share the terrain. In order to move together toward a future we can only imagine, we have to agree on what is here and what is now.

We have to share the concrete if we are to share the abstraction.

My world is so real to me

The words I use to describe it accurate and true

May I not confuse the unique for the universal

Translate yourself to me.

A miscommunication is more than a weakness of
language

It is a missed communion

A missed coming together

A missed reconciliation

May I find the right words

May we share the right experience

May we talk and talk and talk some more

Like children learning a new language,

committed in our curiosity to understand each other
better

May we be fluent in each other

May we reconcile

Come together

Commune

Toward a better future beyond our capacity to name

Perfection

"We must help the child act, think, and will for himself. This is the art of serving the spirit, an art which can be practiced to perfection only when working with children."

- Maria Montessori

What are you becoming?

In your teaching, where did you begin?

Where are you now?

Where are you going?

What is your personal evolution?

I. The Naming of Things: Perfection

The tendency toward Perfection is the consummation of each of the other tendencies: orientation, order, exploration, communication, activity, manipulation, work, repetition, precision, and abstraction. These tendencies compel us to understand more deeply the world we share. They offer us ways of knowing, of placing ourselves in a time, in a context, in a moment, in a relationship. They give us experiences and the means by which to articulate them. The tendency toward Perfection motivates us to refine those experiences, to get it right. The tendency toward Perfection drives us beyond just *being* and toward *becoming*.

Becoming what? Who knows. We are each individually driven to become more than we are now, to become our perfect selves. We are driven to grow, to learn and emerge and propel and improve, to understand that we are never "done." We are never, ever done. Despite the illusions of adulthood, despite how little credit we give each other or ourselves for the ability to change, we are always changing. We are always moving toward something. The tendency toward Perfection implores us to let that be in the direction of good, of peace, of contribution and usefulness, of cooperation and of integrity.

Integrity, from the Latin *integratas,* "intact." Our tendency toward Perfection seeks to make us whole, to help us recover from the injuries, known and unknown, we have endured in this human experiment, to become what it is we can become, whatever it is that we can become.

Our tendency toward Perfection is a divine drive, that spiritual whisper that calls in our ears, "You can do better than this. You can be better than this. We can be better than this." In seeking Perfection, we reach toward a collective horizon, one in which our individual mistakes are shadowed by the overwhelming goodness of our human community.

And we do so with every tool at our disposal. We orient ourselves to know from where our work begins. We seek order to make sense of the work to be done. We explore to find models toward which we are compelled or from which we flee. We communicate to share the experience beyond our singular lives. We are active to put into action those intentions. We manipulate our environments to test the limits of our crafting. We work to develop our usefulness, to contribute to a larger humanity. We repeat to be sure of the work. We seek precision to know what to keep and what to discard. We abstract to articulate, beyond the concrete limits of our lives, the lessons we have learned.

In each tool, we propel ourselves, within our lives, among our lives, beyond our lives, toward a better future we may never see.

The tendency toward Perfection surpasses any of our singular experiences. As we seek it in our individual lives, that seeking contributes to our collective humanity and toward our spiritual evolution. We rely on each of the other tendencies to make sense of the human experience, and the tendency toward Perfection to rise above that experience. The tendency toward Perfection is the tendency of hope, of courage, of the suspension of disbelief. It is the intrinsic drive to endure, despite the damaging or thwarting or eroding experiences of our everyday, despite the very real risk that we will never personally benefit from the evolution. The tendency toward Perfection compels us to strive beyond our human limits and beyond our imaginations toward that complete, intact, best possible self.

II. Perfection and The Child

In the child, we see what we could have become. In the child, we glimpse the future we may be a part of, if we can just get out of its way. Montessorians hold this lesson dearly: the child is perfect. The child is peaceful. The child is naturally motivated to learn, to work, to contribute. And when the child does not demonstrate those natural traits, it is because some obstacle has gotten in her way. What is our role in the process? Simple. Remove the obstacles. Get out of her way.

This is a lofty belief, to be sure. When society outside our classroom challenges us to classify children, to label them earlier and earlier into increasingly narrow boxes, to diagnose them faster and discard them sooner, Montessori offers us a nobler challenge. Look not for the problem with the child. Look for the problem in the environment. Look for the problem in the lesson. Look for the problem in yourself.

We have uncovered the child's capacity for perfection, beyond our own. In order for it to emerge, we must clear the path. We protect the child's potential to reach the sublime by attending first to the pedestrian obstacles in her way. We know they are of our own making. We know that, but for our mistakes, the child would be farther down her own path.

Remember the role of the teacher: scientist, servant, saint. We are called to observe the child like careful scientists, to understand the child's nature, her needs and drives and motivations so that we can help to guide their fulfillment. We are called to be servant to that nature, to prepare an environment within which the right tools, the right materials, the right language and the right opportunities exist. We are called to be saintly, to model what it is we believe is inherent in the child, to serve as a mirror to the child's intrinsic nature as the child learns to articulate it herself.

In that role, as scientist, servant and saint, we are playing make-believe. We are not really what the child can become, not intrinsically in any event. Not anymore. The child is always capable of surpassing us. The child is always filled with more potential than we are. Acknowledging that does nothing to lessen our burden. Indeed, it is because of the child's capacity that we maintain the expectations of ourselves. We may not be able to be perfect, or peaceful, or motivated all the time.

But we can pretend.

We can maintain it in small exchanges, in a few segments of three hours or so at a time. And in the doing, we practice. We may find that we are capable of maintaining the illusion for just a little longer. We may find our betterment less tiring. We may come to be accustomed to acting peacefully, to industry and contribution, to collaboration and cooperation and perfection. We may just be playing a role, but it is the singular role we are called to play in the life of the child. See what the child needs. Provide it to her. And get out of her way.

You are already perfect

You are already peaceful

You are already whole

You need no more than my pure faith in the already

You are already perfect

You are already peaceful

You are already whole

You need no less than my pure faith in the already

You are all ready

Perfect

Peaceful

Whole

III.   Perfection and The Self

Believing ourselves capable of perfection may require a leap of faith, a willing suspension of disbelief. Indeed, we are taught *not* to ask it of ourselves, but rather to be humble and modest and self-effacing. Who are we to strive for our own perfection?

Naming the goal does not, in itself, give us the capacity to reach it. But it gives structure to the possibility. It points us in a direction, even if we know we are unlikely to reach the end of the voyage. And in naming the goal, we mark the distance between where we are and where we hope to be. We identify our need for change, for growth and evolution.

In that sense, believing ourselves capable of perfection is not arrogance, but humility.

We are humble when we acknowledge our imperfections. We are humble when we measure the distance between who we are and who we want to become. In naming perfection as the goal, we claim every fault, every failure, every flaw.

Resigned to the ways in which we've disappointed ourselves, we argue that perfection is an impossible aim. When we name perfection as the goal, we do away with our petty excuses about why it cannot be reached. We are forced, instead, to recognize the ways in which we have fallen short. Humbling, to be sure.

Our tendency toward perfection should not undermine our development. Quite the opposite. Our tendency toward perfection allows us to develop in ways we could not earlier have envisioned.

Likewise, human development is not made purposeful by the attainment of perfection. Once we are perfect, we are no longer human. Our human existence is made purposeful by the efforts we undertake to make it so.

We demonstrate our humanity when we name perfection as our goal. We demonstrate our humanity when we acknowledge that within ourselves which we seek to emend. We demonstrate our humanity to when stop pretending that life is little more than endurance, when we say out loud, "I can do better. I can be better. We can be better." That's when we rise above our animal nature. That's when we move toward the divine. That's when we give some purpose to our endurance, when we begin to forgive ourselves for the endless ways in which we've let ourselves down and begin to become the people we may be capable of becoming.

Seeking perfection allows us to have the experience of the seeking. That we never reach perfection is not the point. To be aware of the seeking, to be aware of the ways in which we could be more decent, more peaceful, more compassionate, more humane with each other, to name the ways in which we might become more selfless, more supportive, more cooperative, more saintly… the seeking is the point. The quest is not made noble by its end, but by the adventures along the way.

I know my failings
Like the back of my hand
They are written in the lines of
my face
In the curve of my shoulders
In the hesitance of my embrace

I know the ways in which I am not
What I hope to be

Let me name the ways in which I am
What I hope to be

I am hopeful
I am human
I am seeking

Every day I begin
I begin again
On the path to what I may
become

Hopeful

Human

Seeking

IV.   Perfection and Each Other

You can probably name the ways in which the people around you remind you of your imperfections. You can probably name the ways in which you remind them of theirs.

Alas. We are much better at identifying what's wrong with ourselves, with each other, with the world, than we are at identifying the ways in which we're doing just fine.

What if...

What if instead of reminding each other of our inadequacies, we made it our habit to name the good? What if instead of focusing on the ways in which we are not who we would like to be, we named what's *right* about who we are and where we are?

We know that none of us will reach perfection in our own lifetimes. Perfection is an evolutionary goal, measured in geologic time. We are moving toward something better, something higher, something closer to the divine. But we are moving in imperceptibly small ways, like water wearing on stone, carving ourselves out in increments invisible to the eye. And just as we may not see the ways in which our humanity moves toward the sublime, we cannot see the ways in which our injuries to each other divert us toward the profane.

We can pretend we are without consequence. We can pretend that the damage we do to each other is not lasting. We can pretend to be resilient. We can pretend we forget. We become so comfortable in the pretending that we come to believe it's real. We become so accustomed to our fractures that we forget that we were supposed to be whole. But unless we acknowledge our fault lines, we can't move past them. We cannot imagine the intact whole. Unless we choose to see what is good in each other, we have no mirrors to see what is worth saving in ourselves.

Perfection, from the Latin *perfectio:* a finishing. We are not perfect at this moment, just as we are not finished. As long as we are alive, we are changing, improving, evolving, becoming. We are never finished. We are constantly refining, polishing, finishing. We serve an essential role in supporting or undermining that work in each other. You can carve your name into metal with a sharp edge, but it takes a soft cloth to bring out the shine. We make lasting impressions through the ways in which we hurt each other, but the recovery from those injuries requires a careful hand, a gentle touch, and a lot of time.

What if......

What if instead of reminding each other of our inadequacies, we made it our habit to name the good? What if instead of focusing on the ways in which we are not who we would like to be, we named what's right? What if instead of defining the tendency toward perfection as a personal, individual drive, we named it as a collective, generational horizon, something toward which we are all moving, something toward which we all strive?

What if...

Seeking your compassion

May I offer you compassion

Seeking your acceptance

May I offer you acceptance

Seeking your reunion

May I offer you reunion

Seeking your hand

May I offer you mine

So we can walk together

Our path is a little less lonely for the company

<u>A Blessing to Another Traveler</u>

Gentle traveler

May your path be peaceful

May your feet find always firm ground

May your burdens be less than your strength

Your strength, greater than your fears

May your eyes and your heart be fixed on the horizon

May you have stillness

And laughter

In equal measure

May you have solace in silent reflection

And comfort in the company of friends

May your true nature

Be your guide

Peace to you on the journey.

Printed in the United States
by Baker & Taylor Publisher Services